NEW SUCCESS *at* FIRST CERTIFICATE

WORKBOOK

NEW SUCCESS *at* FIRST CERTIFICATE

WORKBOOK

Michael Duckworth & Kathy Gude

Oxford University Press

1997

Oxford University Press,
Great Clarendon Street, Oxford OX2 6DP

Oxford New York
Athens Auckland Bangkok Bogota Bombay
Buenos Aires Calcutta Cape Town Dar es Salaam
Delhi Florence Hong Kong Istanbul Karachi
Kuala Lumpur Madras Madrid Melbourne
Mexico City Nairobi Paris Singapore
Taipei Tokyo Toronto

and associated companies in
Berlin Ibadan

OXFORD and OXFORD ENGLISH
are trade marks of Oxford University Press

ISBN 0 19 45 3333 6

Typeset by eMC Design, Bromham, Bedfordshire

Printed in Spain by Mateu Cromo, S.A.

Acknowledgements

The authors and publishers would like to thank the following for permission to reproduce copyright material:

The Reader's Digest Association Limited, Did You Know? © 1990: 'A new song for a new season' and 'Chappe's Signal Success'; Docklands Light Railway: Tourist information leaflet (1991); Voluntary Service Overseas (VSO); © The Observer: 'Making Sense of Monkey Business' by Robien McKie and 'The Meaning of Dreams'; North News: 'Harassment fines for neighbours increased'; "Wall Street" film review by George Perry, Sunday Times 17/9/95; "Climber who 'died'in Mont Blanc Storm" by Richard Duce, Susan Bell and Kate Alderson, The Times 2/9/94 and "Internet traps 'surfers' in addictive web" by Rupert Steiner and Ray Hammond, Sunday Times (Internet) 9/6/96, © Times Newspapers Limited 1996; André Deutsch: The Riches of the Poor by George Mikes (1987); More!: 'What it's like ... Whirlwind Romance'; Landmark Trust: Landmark brochure; Banished Knowledge by Alice Miller published by Virago; The Penguin Group: Down and Out: Orwell's Paris, and London revisited by S. Craig & C. Schwarz; The Fire Protection Association: Fire Protection Leaflet; Leslie Marshall/In Style © 1996 Time Inc.; © Telegraph Group Limited, London, 1995: 'The architects who designed their downfall' by Adrian Berry;The Early Times: 'Ruining the Ruins'; Shelter: 'No Place Like Home'.

Although every effort has been made to trace and contact copyright holders before publication, this has not been possible in the following cases. We apologise for any apparent infringement of copyright and if notified, the publisher will be pleased to rectify any errors or omissions at the earliest opportunity:

Family & Home Security Magazine: 'Good Neighbours'; Living: 'Don't let it happen to your daughter' questionnaire; Miles Kington: Tales of Provincial Life; Channel Four: 'Robotopia'.

Illustrations by:
Richard Draper; Alison Everitt; Martin Cottam; Barrie Mitchell; Technical Graphics Dept. OUP.

The publishers would like to thank the following for permission to reproduce photographs:

J. Southworth/The Photo Co-op; The Landmark Trust.

CONTENTS

UNIT 1

A Reading 1

Read the text and choose the best answer in 1–5.

PLANET EARTH

The planet Earth is 4,600 million years old. It is difficult for us to think about such an enormous length of time because it has little meaning for us. We can, however, simplify the idea to make it more understandable. We can compare the planet Earth to a person of forty-six years of age.

Nothing is known about the first seven years of this person's life. Very little information exists about the middle period either. It was only at the age of forty-two that the Earth began to flower.

Dinosaurs and great reptiles did not appear until one year ago, when the planet was forty-five. Mammals only arrived eight months ago. In the middle of last week, man-like apes became ape-like men and began to communicate with each other. Last weekend, the Ice Age covered the Earth.

Modern man has only been around for four hours. During the last hour man discovered agriculture. The Industrial Revolution and the rise of large cities began just sixty seconds ago.

During that short time, modern man has made a rubbish tip of the Earth. In one minute, he has increased his numbers to terrible proportions, and has caused the death of hundreds of species of animals. He has robbed and destroyed the planet in his search for fuels. Now he stands, like a violent, spoilt child, delighted at the speed of his rise to power, on the edge of the final mass destruction and of killing all the life which exists in the solar system.

1 The passage tells us that
- A a great deal is known about how the Earth was created.
- B life on Earth began relatively recently.
- C more is known about the first part of the Earth's life than the middle part.
- D scientists are well-informed about the middle part of the Earth's life.

2 We are informed by the author that
- A the dinosaurs appeared during the middle period.
- B mammals and great reptiles both appeared at the same time.
- C there were more than forty-five kinds of great reptiles.
- D ape-like men appeared before the last Ice Age.

3 The author is mainly interested in
- A the time when man first evolved from apes.
- B what has happened since the Industrial Revolution.
- C the effects of farming.
- D the period before the last Ice Age.

4 It would appear that the main danger ahead is that
- A man will destroy everything on Earth.
- B man will use up all the fuels.
- C there will be a population explosion.
- D more species of animal may die out.

5 The author's general view of man seems to be that
- A he has no right to be so destructive.
- B he has been the most successful animal.
- C he will be able to control the environment.
- D he has learned a lot from past mistakes.

B Vocabulary 1

Below is a list of animals. Classify them according to the following categories and add three examples of your own.

Mammals	
Birds	
Insects	
Fish	
Reptiles	

chimpanzee	cockroach	salmon	mosquito
eagle	cobra	ant	sardine
whale	robin	tortoise	crocodile
leopard	shark	crow	

C Vocabulary 2

Complete the sentences using the correct form of *say, talk, speak* or *tell*.

1 When the child was in bed, his mother ________ him a story.

2 When she left she ________, 'I'll call again next week.'

3 I've left my watch at home. Could you ________ me the time?

4 What is the word for someone who can ________ two languages fluently?

5 I saw Peter yesterday, and he ________ that he was going to buy a new car.

6 Can you ________ the difference between butter and margarine?

7 What exactly did Jenny ________ to you when you asked her about the party?

8 Sorry, could you ________ up? It's a bad line, and I can't hear very well.

9 Don't be silly. I wasn't angry. I don't know what you are ________ about.

10 Excuse me, could you ________ me the way to the station?

D Use of English 1

Complete the text using the given words. There is an example at the beginning (0).

said say speak told (x2)
who (x2) which whose (x3)

Dian Fossey, (0) *whose* life story was (1)________ in the film *Gorillas In The Mist*, was an American zoologist (2)________ lived among the mountain gorillas of Rwanda for eighteen years. The relationship they built up allowed her to observe them in more detail than ever before. In the end, she could sit safely near adult gorillas and their children while she was making her notes.

She set up the Karisoke Research Centre, one of (3)________ aims was to protect gorillas from poachers (4)________ killed them for their skins, and her work allowed the gorilla population to rise from about 240 to 600. She herself was killed in 1985, and people (5)________ the crime was committed by a poacher (6)________ business was being damaged by her work.

The studies she carried out have encouraged other scientists to look at gorillas' intelligence. They cannot, of course, (7)________ a language, but there are ways in (8)________ they can communicate with each other. One researcher (9)________ a conference that he had taught a gorilla sign language, and he (10)________ that it was able to learn over 100 different signs.

E Use of English 2

Complete the text with the correct form of the words in capitals. There is an example at the beginning (0).

The songs of the humpback whale are beautiful (0) *collections* of moans and sighs and it is possible to make (1)__________ of these with a microphone. With enough (2)__________, you can listen to a song and tell which year it was sung in and where it came from.

The whales do most of their (3)__________ in the winter season, after their annual (4)__________ south from the Arctic. It is always the young males who set off first to the tropical breeding areas, and most of the (5)__________ are given by solitary males who are looking for a mate.

The songs all have a definite sequence of parts. This (6)__________ is never changed, and there are clear rules of (7)__________ which must not be broken. There is very little (8)__________ between the songs at the start of a season and those from the previous year. However, over the next few months, the different parts of each song may be swapped, shortened, and (9)__________ may be made to the notes. During a breeding season, the whales all try to sing the most up-to-date version of the song. This (10)__________ is similar to the way human language evolves, with contributions from many members of the population.

0 COLLECT
1 RECORD
2 PRACTISE
3 SING
4 MIGRATE
5 PERFORM
6 ARRANGE
7 COMPOSE
8 DIFFER
9 ALTER
10 DEVELOP

F Vocabulary 3

Complete the sentences using the correct form of these phrasal verbs or verbs with prepositions.

go on go up look up look into come down

1 Jenny's upstairs, but she'll ________ ________ soon.

2 They ________ ________ and waved at the helicopter.

3 The inquiry team are ________ ________ exactly why the accident happened.

4 I can't remember her number. Could you ________ it ________ in the phone book for me?

5 At the end of the concert, the audience ________ ________ clapping until the singer came back and did an encore.

6 When they ________ ________ the nest, they saw three baby birds.

7 When I last visited the Eiffel Tower, the lift wasn't working, so I ________ ________ the stairs.

8 Although unemployment is high, the government say it will ________ ________ soon.

9 When he went to the fair, Jimmy wanted to ________ ________ the big wheel.

10 He was pleased to hear that the value of his house had ________ ________ since he had bought it.

G Use of English 3

Read the letter from a student at a language school to an English-speaking friend. If a line is correct, put a tick (✓). If a line has an unnecessary word, underline it. There are two examples at the beginning (0) and (00).

0 This is just a quick note to tell to you that I am fine and
00 that the course is going well. I am in the top class, ✓
1 and I'm having a great time. There are eight of us in
2 the class, all from different countries, so we have to
3 speak with English all the time.
4 I wanted to say you how pleased I am with the school,
5 and I am really glad that you told to me about it.
6 The facilities are great and our social life is wonderful.
7 We have the parties twice a month, and every weekend
8 we also have the chance to go on to all sorts of interesting
9 excursions which they are organized by the school.
10 They've also got tennis courts, but we'll have to wait
11 until it stops to raining before we get the chance to play!
12 Anyway, I'd love for to see you again, and my host
13 family have said that you are welcome to stay in the
14 spare room. So please tell me that if you think you'll
15 be able to come down in here, and I'll sort things out.
Hope to see you again soon.

H Reading 2

Read the text on the right about the invention of semaphore. Five sentences have been removed. Choose from sentences A–F the one which fits each gap (1–4). There is one extra sentence which you do not need. There is an example at the beginning (0).

A Using ropes, these could be moved to form 49 different shapes that could be recognized easily.

B The main problem was that it could not be used during the night or on foggy days.

C These messages could be sent very quickly.

D The new republic faced enemies on all sides in the form of the forces of Britain, Austria, Holland, Prussia and Spain.

E In August 1794, it carried its first message, the news of Napoleon's victory at Le Quenoy.

F A system was built between London and the south coast, and other countries followed.

War has been called 'the mother of invention', and this was certainly true in the French Revolutionary wars in 1792. [0 *D*] What the Revolutionary Government urgently needed was a reliable system of communication.

Claude Chappe, who was a priest and an engineer, had developed a telegraph system, but had not been able to test it fully. However, his brother Ignace was a member of the government, and arranged for Claude's system to be tested. It turned out to be a great success and started a new form of high-speed communication.

The two brothers had a series of towers built 5 to 10 km apart. At the top of each tower was a tall wooden mast, and they attached one horizontal and two vertical wooden beams to this mast. [1] Claude called this system 'semaphore', which comes from the Greek meaning 'bearing a sign'.

Operators in each tower watched neighbouring towers through a telescope and then passed the message on to the next one in the line. The first line stretched from Paris to Lille, a distance of 230 km. [2] At an average speed of three signals a minute, it was carried in 20 minutes, more than 90 times faster than messengers on horseback.

Once the value of Chappe's system was understood, it soon became the standard method of communication in Europe. [3] By the time the electric telegraph was developed, France had more than 550 semaphore towers stretching 4,800km.

Unfortunately, Chappe's system had some disadvantages. [4] The towers were also expensive to maintain and the cost of staff was high. In the end, Chappe was depressed by these criticisms of his inventions and by claims from other engineers that they had invented semaphore, and he committed suicide in 1805.

UNIT 2

A Reading 1

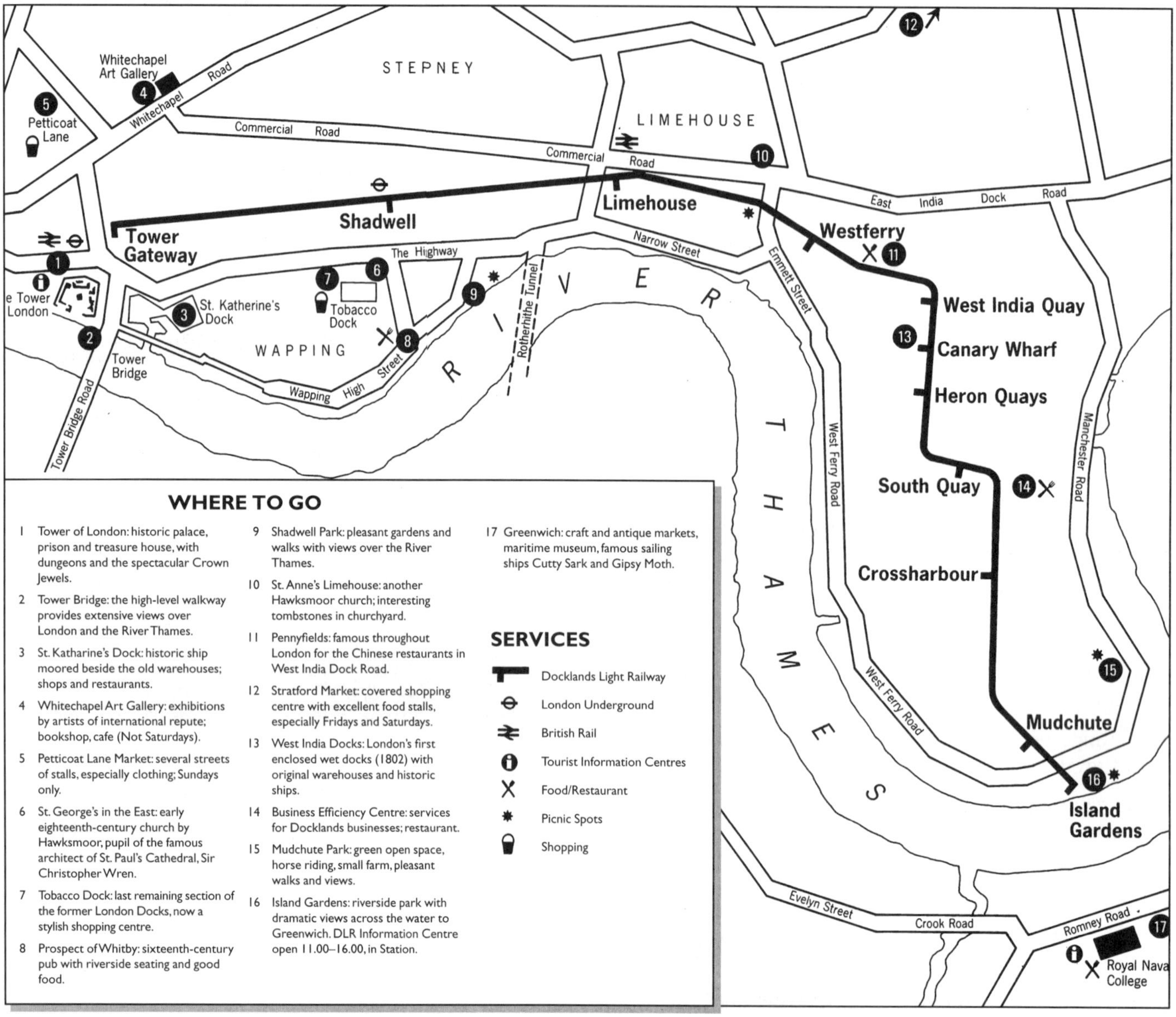

WHERE TO GO

1 Tower of London: historic palace, prison and treasure house, with dungeons and the spectacular Crown Jewels.

2 Tower Bridge: the high-level walkway provides extensive views over London and the River Thames.

3 St. Katharine's Dock: historic ship moored beside the old warehouses; shops and restaurants.

4 Whitechapel Art Gallery: exhibitions by artists of international repute; bookshop, cafe (Not Saturdays).

5 Petticoat Lane Market: several streets of stalls, especially clothing; Sundays only.

6 St. George's in the East: early eighteenth-century church by Hawksmoor, pupil of the famous architect of St. Paul's Cathedral, Sir Christopher Wren.

7 Tobacco Dock: last remaining section of the former London Docks, now a stylish shopping centre.

8 Prospect of Whitby: sixteenth-century pub with riverside seating and good food.

9 Shadwell Park: pleasant gardens and walks with views over the River Thames.

10 St. Anne's Limehouse: another Hawksmoor church; interesting tombstones in churchyard.

11 Pennyfields: famous throughout London for the Chinese restaurants in West India Dock Road.

12 Stratford Market: covered shopping centre with excellent food stalls, especially Fridays and Saturdays.

13 West India Docks: London's first enclosed wet docks (1802) with original warehouses and historic ships.

14 Business Efficiency Centre: services for Docklands businesses; restaurant.

15 Mudchute Park: green open space, horse riding, small farm, pleasant walks and views.

16 Island Gardens: riverside park with dramatic views across the water to Greenwich. DLR Information Centre open 11.00–16.00, in Station.

17 Greenwich: craft and antique markets, maritime museum, famous sailing ships Cutty Sark and Gipsy Moth.

SERVICES

- Docklands Light Railway
- London Underground
- British Rail
- Tourist Information Centres
- Food/Restaurant
- Picnic Spots
- Shopping

Look at the information and the map showing the Docklands Light Railway (DLR) above then match the places 0–7 below with the comments A–H on the next page. There is an example at the beginning (0).

Petticoat Lane Market	0 *E*	South Quay	4
Tobacco Dock	1	Mudchute	5
Westferry	2	Island Gardens	6
Stratford Market	3	The Royal Naval College	7

A You can learn about the history of sea travel here.

B If you need business services, this is the place to get off.

C You won't get wet here if it rains.

D If you like elegant shops, this is the place to visit.

E You'll find lots to wear on display here.

F Here you can get up-to-date travel information about the DLR.

G This is where to get off the train if you like Chinese food.

H You might enjoy getting off here if you like animals!

B Reading 2

Now read the history of the Docklands Light Railway and choose the best answer in 1–4.

The History of the Railway

The Docklands Light Railway (DLR) took just three years to build at a cost of £77 million. It is London's first Light Rail System, but its route follows that of a number of older lines, even using the

original cuttings and brick viaducts which carried the nineteenth century railways through the crowded districts of the East End.

The section of line from Tower Gateway station to Poplar follows the line of one of London's earliest railways, the London & Blackwell (1840), a cable-hauled railway (later converted to steam) which carried passengers to steam ships at Blackwell Pier, and provided transport for the messengers and clerks who went backwards and forwards between the docks and the city every day.

From Poplar to Island Gardens, a new line crosses high above the dock waters, then joins the old track of the Millwall Extension Railway, built to service the Millwall Docks (1868) and to provide transport for workers in the local factories. This line was horse-drawn for part of its route, until the 1880s.

The Poplar to Stratford section of the DLR route was first developed by the North London Railway, built in the 1850s to link the West and East India Docks with the manufacturing districts of the Midlands and North of England. There were major railway works and sidings at Bow until recently.

The trains are automatically controlled from a central computer, which deals with all signalling and other safety factors, as well as adjusting speeds to keep within the timetable; on board each vehicle, Train Captains, who are also fully qualified drivers, are equipped with two-way radios to maintain contact with central control. There are passenger lifts, and self-service ticket machines, at every station.

For further information about the DLR, please consult your Train Captain, or call at the Island Gardens Station or ring 0171-222 1234.

1 The history tells us that the DLR
- A was begun in the nineteenth century.
- B will be finished in three years' time.
- C follows some of the original line.
- D took three years longer than expected to complete.

2 We are informed that the London and Blackwell railway
- A now carries many passengers to and from the docks.
- B was a busy line a few years ago.
- C used to employ many messengers and clerks.
- D was not originally a steam railway.

3 It appears that the Poplar to Stratford section of the DLR route was originally developed to
- A promote travel in England.
- B encourage trade abroad.
- C create employment.
- D make the transport of goods easier.

4 The trains on the DLR are controlled by
- A a computer based elsewhere.
- B drivers on the trains themselves.
- C two-way radios operated by the drivers.
- D a computer on board the train.

C Vocabulary 1

Choose a suitable word from the list to complete the text below. There are three words you do not need. There is an example at the beginning (0).

travel	flight	excursion
trip	journey	tour
visit	voyage	expedition
ride	drive	crossing

It was very foggy and our (0) *flight* from London had arrived two hours late. We finally got out of the airport at 8 in the evening. We had arranged to go on a guided (1)________ of the city at night but we realized that we were going to miss it, as it is at least a half an hour's (2)________ from the airport to the centre of Paris. We had also booked a day-(3)________ to Versailles the next morning but, after our long (4)________, we knew it was going to be difficult to get up early! I suppose we could have gone by ferry, but after we'd had a particularly rough (5)________ two years ago, we said 'Never again!'. We both love to (6)________ and (7)________ other countries. In fact, one of our greatest ambitions is to join a group of explorers and go on a(n) (8)________ to the Himalayas!

D Language study

Read the conversation and put *may, should, must* or *will* into the correct spaces. In some cases, more than one answer may be possible. There is an example at the beginning (0).

Passenger: Excuse me! (0) *May* I leave my suitcases here for a moment? (1)_____ that be all right?

Clerk: I'm afraid not. You (2)_____ keep your luggage with you at all times.

Passenger: But I can't carry it round all the time. It's far too heavy!

Clerk: You (3)_____ get a trolley.

Passenger: And where (4)_____ I find one of these trolleys?

Clerk: You (5)_____ find one just outside the main entrance.

Passenger: I suppose I (6)_____ have to go and look for one myself.

Clerk: Well, if you wait a moment, I (7)_____ see if I can call a porter for you.

Passenger: Thank you very much. I really (8)_____ buy myself some wheels for my suitcases. That (9)_____ be the answer to my problems.

E Vocabulary 2

Use either *give* or *take* in its correct form to complete the sentences below.

Example:

If you fancy getting away from it all, why not *take* a two-day city break?

1 ________ your time. There's no rush!

2 Could you ________ me a lift to the station?

3 When you reach home, ________ me a call.

4 When they heard he was leaving, they ________ him a farewell party.

5 All the children ________ part in the end-of-term school concert.

6 It ________ me a long time to get to work yesterday morning.

7 I have been asked to ________ a talk about how to prepare students for examinations.

8 A woman ________ birth to a baby boy while on a flight to Australia yesterday.

9 Could you ________ care of my luggage while I get a cup of coffee?

10 Organizing this trip has ________ me a lot of trouble.

F Vocabulary 3

Arrange these words in five groups of six words each. Each group should contain words which are related to each other. Do you know what they all mean?

tube	liner	motorbike	handbag
suitcase	track	luggage	journey
harbour	line	excursion	path
station	trip	airport	holdall
outing	port	docks	quay
rucksack	lane	briefcase	drive
taxi	jet	hovercraft	route
tour	way		

____

____

____

____

____

G Vocabulary 4

Complete the crossword with words connected with *travel*. The numbers in brackets tell you the number of letters in the missing words.

ACROSS

1 You must know this before boarding a plane. (6,6)
6 It's useful if you want to find your way in a strange city. (3)
8 A one-way ticket. (6)
9 'Have you anything to ______?' asked the customs officer. (7)
11 'Because of the bad weather conditions there will be a slight ______ before our take-off.' (5)
12 Opposite of 8 across. (6)
13 You might be lucky and get one next to the window. (4)
15 The capital of Italy. (4)
16 'You must pay us a ______ on your next trip.'(5)
17 You can leave your bags there. (4-7)

DOWN

2 'We apologise for the ______ of flight BA123 from Madrid.' (4,7)
3 'Flight OA124 is now boarding at ______ 7.' (4)
4 'The next train ______ arrive at Platform 7 will be the 8.45 from Liverpool.' (2)
5 Make sure you do not exceed the allowance for this. (7)
7 It's quicker to travel by ______.(5)
9 Goods which can be bought cheaply. (4-4)
10 You go through this after Passport Control. (7)
13 A ______-voyage. (3)
14 They say it broadens the mind. (6)

H Use of English

Read the text and decide which word, A, B, C or D, best fits each space. There is an example at the beginning (0).

I arrived at the airport with plenty of time to check (0) *in* . It was a trip I had done many times before and, (1)______ to the clerk at the desk, there were no problems and the (2)______ was scheduled to leave on time. I was flying to Thessaloniki but I had to (3)______ planes in Athens. Suddenly there was a(n) (4)______ saying that, because of a strike by air-traffic controllers, the plane would be (5)______ by at least two hours. I headed in the (6)______ of the restaurant. After an interminable wait of about six hours, tired and frustrated, we eventually (7)______ the plane. When we (8)______ in Athens, it was almost midnight, and there was no sign of any connection to Thessaloniki.

0	A up	B into
	C in	D through
1	A referring	B relating
	C according	D conforming
2	A journey	B travel
	C trip	D flight
3	A transfer	B alter
	C change	D exchange
4	A advertisement	B broadcast
	C announcement	D notice
5	A checked	B stopped
	C delayed	D postponed
6	A way	B direction
	C route	D path
7	A joined	B boarded
	C took	D caught
8	A arrived	B got
	C came	D went

UNIT 3

A Reading 1

Read the information about VSO and choose the best answer in 1–5.

Voluntary Service Overseas

VSO

VSO is a registered charity dedicated to assisting in developing countries. More specifically, it is a recruitment agency which finds, selects and places volunteers in response to overseas requests.

This work makes it distinctive among other charities and organizations in the UK. It sends people, not money, so that its services are, in effect, entirely complementary to the efforts being made by agencies like Oxfam, Christian Aid and Save the Children Fund with whom it often works directly.

VSO tries to respond to requests from overseas which ask for volunteers. Its bias is firmly towards the poorest members of the community and it takes great care to avoid undermining job opportunities for local people.

Both staff and volunteers also pay special attention to women's roles in development projects. This is because women's roles in child-rearing, in education and community cohesion are essential in any healthy process of change.

Over the past 38 years, more than 21,000 volunteers have worked abroad with VSO. There are now over 1,900 volunteers working in 59 of the less developed countries in Africa, Asia, the Pacific and the Caribbean.

The application of each volunteer is carefully considered in order to select and interview candidates against each job request from the field, to seek the person with the right blend of skills and personality.

VSO, the work

VSO volunteers do not go to developing countries as visiting experts with all the answers. It is always a process of sharing and learning. The aim is that when the volunteer returns home, there exists a community with a stronger sense of independence and self-reliance... and a volunteer with a new understanding and appreciation of life and people everywhere. The range of jobs required of VSO is wide – reflecting the needs of any society in the modern world.

1 VSO is different from other charities and organizations in the UK because it
A is a registered body.
B sends financial aid to developing countries.
C sends volunteers to help abroad.
D recruits volunteers to work in Britain.

2 Requests from overseas most likely to be dealt with are those which
A specifically ask for female staff and volunteers.
B require volunteers to work with the local inhabitants.
C require help and advice on health care.
D need help to train less wealthy members of the community.

3 According to those who work for VSO, who plays the most important part in bringing about change?
A charitable organizations
B volunteers from abroad
C women in local communities
D staff who recruit volunteers

4 What happens when VSO wants to appoint new volunteers?
A They give preference to applicants living abroad.
B They give each applicant several interviews.
C They refer applications to countries requesting volunteers.
D They match all applicants to jobs very carefully.

5 The volunteer chosen to go out to a developing country
A must have experience of working overseas.
B will quickly become an expert in the field.
C will gain more knowledge about the world we live in.
D must leave the country before it becomes independent.

B Vocabulary 1

Jobs can be grouped into different categories. Match the categories (1–8) with the jobs (A–T) below. You may use your dictionary.

1 Forestry
2 Fisheries
3 Agriculture
4 Education and Librarianship
5 Health
6 Business and Commerce
7 Community and Social Development
8 Technical Trades, Crafts and Engineering

A Community workers
B Computer programmers
C Fishermen
D Teachers
E Carpenters
F Business entrepreneurs
G Health educators
H Agricultural engineers
I Mechanics
J Accountants
K Town planners
L Doctors
M Tree preservationists
N Librarians
O Social workers
P Boat builders
Q Computer analysts
R Technical teachers
S Building instructors
T Tree surgeons

C Writing

Write a letter to an organization you would like to work for, asking them to send you details of any vacancies they may have.

D Phrasal verbs

Replace the words in italics with a suitable phrasal verb with *come* in its correct form.

come: *across* / *up* / *down with* / *up against* / *about* / *to*

Example:
Have you *found* the invoices I asked you to find yesterday?
come across

1 I'm afraid we're going to *face* a lot of problems trying to introduce this new system.
2 The new project *was mentioned* at the directors' meeting last week.
3 The room was so hot that a man actually fainted. Luckily he *regained consciousness* almost immediately.
4 One of the secretaries has *developed* a nasty cold and won't be in today.
5 What I want to know is how the accident *happened*.
6 Where on earth did you *find* this beautiful, old desk?

E Use of English

Read Mary's letter to Paul about her new job. If a line is correct, put a tick (✓). If a line has an unnecessary word, underline it. There are two examples at the beginning (0) and (00).

Dear Paul,

0 I am writing to tell you that I have been appointed ✓
00 for Operations Manager at the City Zoo. The zoo is a
1 major of tourist attraction, with over a million visitors
2 a year. I shall be the responsible for looking after
3 the visitors and the zoo by itself. They were looking
4 for candidates between twenty-eight and forty-five.
5 They also wanted that someone with managerial ability
6 and relevant experience. Surprisingly, I got the job!
7 Accommodation is also provided, so we won't be need
8 to look for somewhere to live. My starting salary'll
9 be around £25,000, which isn't bad! I'm really
10 looking forward to starting out work there. I hope
11 I'll be able to cope with all the work I involved!
12 I must admit I'm a little so nervous about it all!
13 Hope to see you sometime soon. Love to the family.
Best wishes,
Mary

F Vocabulary 2

Read part of a letter to colleagues about interviewing candidates for a job and fill in the missing words, which are all connected with work. The first letter of each word is given.

Example:

A c*areer* in this field can be very hard work but it is rewarding.

We advertised the (1) p__________ of Sales Manager last week in the national newspapers. So far we've had more than fifty (2) a__________ for the job. As you know, we're offering a (3) s__________ of £19,000. We would prefer to appoint someone with a few years' (4) e__________ in the field. Remember that we stated in the advertisement that high academic (5) q__________ are not so necessary for a job like this. We need to stress that in this company all (6) e__________ are treated in the same way. All staff are entitled to an annual share in the (7) p__________ of the company, and we believe that good working relations between (8) m__________ and (9) s__________ are essential. We've selected ten (10) c__________ to be interviewed next week. The successful candidate will take up his/her (11) a__________ from next month.

G Language study

Match the phrases on the left with the meanings they express on the right. Draw lines between the pairs.

Are you going to (do?)	a request
Is it going to (do)?	intention
Will you (do)?	probability
Will you be (doing)?	something that will be in progress in the future
Would you (do)?	

Write sentences using the expressions above and following the instructions in sentences 1–8.

1 Ask someone to open a window.

____

2 Ask if someone intends to have a quiet evening in.

____

3 Ask if someone has made arrangements for attending the next committee meeting.

____

4 Ask if there is any probability of it raining this afternoon.

____

5 Ask if someone intends to tell the truth.

____

6 Ask if there is any likelihood of interest rates rising again.

____

7 Ask someone to post a letter for you.

____

8 Ask if someone has arranged to go abroad for their holiday this year.

____

H Reading 2

Read these job advertisements. Which of the advertisements A–D states the following? Some of the statements appear in more than one advertisement.

There is an example at the beginning (0).

You must be understanding.	0 *A*	
You need to know something about computers.	1	2
You need to be good at marketing.	3	
You should be able to get on with all sorts of people.	4	
You must be able to work under stress.	5	
You will have to work evenings and weekends.	6	
You need to be a good communicator.	7	
You need to be interested in nature.	8	9
You must be able to drive.	10	11
You will earn more money if you have a few years' experience.	12	
You should have some experience of office work.	13	
You will have a three-year contract.	14	

A

Challenging, rewarding experiences

Morton Social Services require staff who are committed to providing a sensitive service for our community.

CHILDREN & FAMILIES (CARE)

Qualified Social Workers

Can you meet the Morton Challenge?

We wish to recruit energetic Qualified Social Workers with experience of care work, who can deal with the pressure of working in a busy Area Office. We are committed to raising standards and promoting professional practice in an Equal Opportunities environment. Your Application should reflect your knowledge as indicated in the person specification.

Applicants with four years' post-qualification experience in a social worker graded post will be guaranteed a salary of at least £18,400.

B

International Wildlife Organization I.W.O.

REGIONAL ORGANIZER

Salary Circa £14,000

To raise funds and promote environmental awareness in the North

IWO is a leading international wildlife organization.

- Can you demonstrate an interest in local and international environmental issues?
- Do you have practical experience of managing and motivating volunteers?
- Do you have practical experience of word processing? This post includes considerable administration using a PC.
- Can you work well with a wide variety of people, have patience, a sense of humour and enjoy public speaking?
- Are you willing to work unconventional hours including a considerable number of evenings and weekends?
- Do you have a full current Driving Licence?

Benefits include use of a car, four weeks' paid annual leave, all normal expenses and a non-contributory pension scheme. Office equipment will be provided.

If you answer YES to all of these questions, and live within the region specified, please apply for an application form and further details.

C

UNIVERSITY OF HOLDSWORTH
Academic Investment Department

ASSISTANT TO THE DIRECTOR

We need an experienced and enthusiastic person to assist the Director in securing funds for the University from external sources including charitable trusts, industry and individuals and to provide administrative and secretarial support to ensure the efficient running of this small and energetic Department.

Experience of office administration and computer skills, including word-processing, databases and spreadsheets are essential, as are strong verbal and written communication skills. Experience of fund-raising/public relations an advantage. Appointment for one year in the first instance. Salary £15,000 per annum.

The University is committed to an Equal Opportunities Policy Promoting excellence in education and research.

D

NORTH MONKSHIRE FOREST

PROJECT DIRECTOR

£20,500 per annum

The North Monkshire Forest belongs to the people, businesses and landowners of the area. As Project Director you will have overall responsibility to these people and the partner organizations for the development of this unique forest and management of its project team.

You are someone with experience, who can demonstrate a high level of management, marketing and environmental awareness. You will already have achieved results in other land management schemes and can bring this drive and experience to the North Monkshire Forest.

The appointment will be for three years. It will include car user allowance, assisted car purchase and relocation expenses.

For an informal discussion about the post and the project, please telephone Frank Meadows on 01432 707332.

UNIT 4

A Reading

Read the article about the meaning of dreams. Choose the most suitable heading from the list (A–I) for each part of the article (1–7). There is one heading which you do not need. There is an example at the beginning (0).

THE MEANING OF DREAMS

We all have dreams and can often remember parts or images from them. Here is a guide to the meanings of the most common images that appear in dreams.

0 *H*

This is one of the most common images, typically showing insecurity and anxiety. It may relate to a fear that a career or a relationship is coming to an end. The fact that we are not hurt when we land represents a hope that things won't turn out too badly.

1 ____

This common dream – which commonly involves using our own arm or leg power (rather than any kind of engine) – seems to represent a wish to escape from the problems we are facing in everyday life. It may also represent a wish to achieve greater power.

2 ____

This represents strength and power. If the dreamers are inside, they are protected by the thick walls. If they are outside and looking at it, they may desire that safety. It is also sometimes the symbol of a woman.

3 ____

This suggests that the dreamer has mixed feelings of love and hostility towards the person who dies, particularly if that person is close. If dreamers see themselves die, this may represent a desire to escape from pressure.

4 ____

Anxiety dreams are very common when something is worrying us. We are being put to the test. The mind remembers times in the past when we were nervous, and a common image is that of a test for which we were badly prepared.

5 ____

This is naturally associated with passion and love, and, not surprisingly, the dangers that go with them. In many cases it shows that the dreamer is both attracted to passion but afraid of being burned.

6 ____

Running forwards and not getting anywhere, or trying to walk through water or honey is a common image in dreams. It symbolizes a conflict of feeling, particularly the desire to escape, yet at the same time, not to escape.

7 ____

These represent obstacles and difficulties which the dreamers feel they have to overcome. If the dreamers keep on climbing without getting anywhere, it could be that they are chasing goals that they cannot hope to achieve.

A FIRE
B CASTLE
C DEATH
D MOUNTAINS
E EXAMS
F WILD ANIMALS
G FLYING
H FALLING
I GETTING STUCK

B Vocabulary 1

Find a word in the text which means:

1 mental pictures or ideas ________
2 a feeling of uncertainty or helplessness ________
3 something that represents an idea ________
4 unfriendly or angry feeling ________
5 a strong wish ________
6 a very powerful feeling ________
7 things which get in your way ________
8 running after ________

C Language study 1

Rewrite these sentences using *few* or *little*. Use the word in bold.

1 I can get by on hardly any money.

very

I can get by ______________ money.

2 I need to discuss some things with you.

few

There ______________ we need to discuss.

3 Hardly anyone came to the meeting.

very

There ______________ at the meeting.

4 One or two people said they couldn't come to the party.

few

There ______________ who said they couldn't come to the party.

5 Yes, I'll give you a hand. I've got some time to spare.

little

Yes, I'll give you a hand. I've got ______________ to spare.

6 I hardly have any friends.

very

I have ______________ friends.

D Vocabulary 2

Complete the sentences with a word from the list.

daydream	nightmare	illusion	reality
hallucination	imagination	horror	fantasy

1 They don't tell you what happens at the end of the film. You have to use your ______________.

2 Living in the South of France sounded wonderful, but in ______________ we had a lot of problems.

3 In her English lesson, Ann sat at the back of the classroom and looked out of the window, lost in a(n) ______________.

4 In the picture, this line looks longer than the other, but in fact they're the same. It's an optical ______________.

5 She woke up screaming because she had just had a terrible ______________.

6 The patient was having a(n) ______________, because she thought the psychiatrist was holding a snake, not a pen.

7 It's time you stopped living in your ______________ world and started to face facts.

8 There's a good ______________ film on tonight about two people who come back from the dead and start murdering everyone they used to know.

E Language study 2

The table shows the most important tense changes from direct to reported speech. Complete the table by filling in the spaces in the right-hand column.

DIRECT SPEECH			REPORTED SPEECH
I know quite a lot of people here.	Simple present	► Simple past	*He said that he (1)* knew *quite a lot of people there.*
John is feeling much better.	Present continuous	► Past continuous	*He said that John (2)* was feeling *much better.*
I enjoyed my holiday in the States.	Simple past	► Past perfect	*He said that he (3)* had enjoyed *his holiday in the States.*
Jackie wasn't feeling very well.	Past continuous	► Past perfect continuous	*He said that Jackie (4)* hadn't been feeling *very well.*
They've seen the Eiffel Tower.	Present perfect	► Past perfect	*He said that they (5)* had seen *the Eiffel Tower.*
I've been waiting for ages.	Present perfect continuous	► Past perfect continuous	*He said that he (6)* had been waiting *for ages.*
Nobody had warned them about the storm.	Past perfect	► Past perfect	*He said that nobody (7)* had warned them *about the storm.*
I'd been wanting to see you.	Past perfect continuous	► Past perfect continuous	*He said that he (8)* had been wanting *to see me.*
will, can, may, shall, must this, today, tomorrow, here	Other changes	► Other changes	*would, (9)* could, might, should, had to *that, (10)* that day, the next day, there

F Language study 3

Rewrite the passage below using reported speech.

'My name's Vera and I came over from East Berlin just after the fall of the Wall, and I've been living in London since then. In Berlin I was a journalist, but now I am working for the BBC and I really enjoy it. I'm not sure if I will go back to live in Germany. I was thinking about going back to visit my family in May, because I haven't seen them for a long time but they have said they would quite like to come to London instead.'

I met an interesting woman the other day. She said her name was Vera, and that she (1) had come over from East Berlin just after the fall of the Wall, and she (2) had been living in London since then. In Berlin she (3) had been a journalist, but now (4) was working for the BBC and she really (5) enjoyed it. She said she (6) wasn't sure if she (7) would go back to live in Germany. She told me that she (8) had been thinking about going back to visit her family in May, because she (9) had seen them for a long time but they (10) had said they would quite like to come to London instead.

G Phrasal verbs

Complete the sentences with the correct form of one of these phrasal verbs.

take over	run into	look up
take up	take in	look into
run through	run over	look forward to

1 The government have set up an enquiry to ________ the causes of the oil disaster.

2 We've got a smaller table in the kitchen now because the old one ________ far too much space.

3 Mandy's very upset because she ________ her cat last week while she was driving into her garage.

4 I've been very tired at work, so I'm really ________ going away on holiday next week.

5 The course is quite hard – there's just so much new information to ________.

6 The pilot ________ difficulties, and had to return to the airport for an emergency landing.

7 If you're not sure how to use a phrasal verb, ______ it ______ in the dictionary.

8 When the company was ________, the new bosses made a lot of people redundant.

9 Let's ________ the arrangements for tomorrow's visit so that we all know what we are meant to do.

H Use of English 1

Complete the text about a dream with the words below. There is an example at the beginning (0).

saw	if	told	had
very	a	refuses	about
find	made	who	had
so	was	falling	into

I am a pop singer and I've (0) *made* a lot of money this year because I've had (1)________ few number one records. But my relationship with my boyfriend Jim, (2)________ is also my manager, has run (3)________ difficulties. We seem to have (4)________ little in common, because everything has changed. I've tried to discuss the problems, but he just gets angry and (5)________ to talk (6)________ it. And I've met another man, Paul, and I (7)________ him very attractive.

Anyway, the other night I (8)________ a strange dream. I was with Jim, and we were walking along a path at the top of a cliff. It was a windy day, and suddenly there was a gust of wind that was (9)________ strong that we were both blown off the cliff. I thought I (10)________ going to die, but just before I hit the ground, I stopped (11)________ and somehow landed safely on my feet. But then I saw Jim, and he was dead. It was cold and dark and I ran down the beach. Then I (12)________ Paul sitting by a fire, so I ran to him and sat down next to him to get warm. He asked me (13)________ I was all right, and I said I was fine. Then I (14)________ him what (15)________ happened, and we kissed. Then I woke up.

I Language study 4

Match what the speaker is doing in sentences 1–8 with the reporting verbs below. Write 1–8 next to each verb.

promising	_____	telling	_____
agreeing	_____	asking	_____
denying	_____	admitting	_____
refusing	_____	advising	_____

1 Yes, I'm afraid it was me who took the money.

2 I had absolutely nothing to do with the robbery. I wasn't even in the country.

3 OK, I'll help you with your composition if you help me with the grammar.

4 No, I'm sorry but I will not help you this time.

5 I think that, if I were you, I would talk to her and tell her about your feelings.

6 Put your name and candidate number on the answer sheet, but don't turn over the question paper yet.

7 I won't ever forget you, and I'll write every day.

8 Could you turn your music down, please?

J Use of English 2

Rewrite these sentences using the word in bold.

1 My father says he won't lend me the money I need.

to

My father _______________ me the money I need.

2 My boss said to me :'Please come in and sit down.'

asked

My boss _______________ and sit down.

3 I'd like to see some galleries, but not many.

few

There are _______________ would like to see.

4 I've found a great site on the Internet.

come

I've _______________ a great site on the Internet.

5 The thief said: 'I didn't steal the car.'

stealing

The thief _______________ the car.

6 The doctor said to me: 'If I were you, I wouldn't smoke.'

advised

The doctor _______________ smoke.

7 He said the petrol tank was empty.

run

He said that _______________ petrol.

8 While I was looking at him, he fired the gun.

saw

I _______________ the gun.

9 I can't wait to see all my old friends again.

forward

I _______________ all my old friends again.

10 I asked him: 'Did you enjoy yourself in Spain?'

had

I asked him _______________ a good time in Spain.

UNIT 5

A Reading

Read the text and choose the best answer in 1–5.

Good Neighbours

The 'Neighbourhood Watch' scheme all started a few years ago in the quiet village of Mollington after a number of burglaries in the village and the surrounding area. The residents of the village came up with the idea that they themselves could keep an eye on their neighbours' property while they were away on holiday. Since then, and with the support of the government and police, more than 50,000 'Neighbourhood Watch' schemes have been set up all over the country.

The object of each 'Watch' group is to reduce the opportunities that criminals have in any particular street or area. Each resident who is a member of the scheme agrees to call the police whenever they see something suspicious. Everything is done calmly and discreetly – it is the police who actually check out each report and investigate what is happening. Residents who are part of the 'Watch' are not supposed to act as police or put themselves in any danger.

When a new Neighbourhood Watch scheme is set up in an area, the first thing people notice is the large, brightly coloured 'Neighbourhood Watch' sign. This is a great deterrent to most burglars and vandals, because very few of them will take a chance of breaking into someone's house if they know that there is a high risk of being seen by neighbours keeping a look-out. Burglars also know that people who are part of 'Neighbourhood Watch' schemes are more likely to have fitted good locks to their doors and windows.

There's another benefit too. In the time since the 'Neighbourhood Watch' scheme came into existence, there is growing evidence of a new community spirit. It is bringing people together as never before, and encouraging people to care for each other. New friendships are being made, and contact is often established with old people living on their own, who are often the most frightened and the most at risk.

1 The 'Neighbourhood Watch' scheme in Mollington was started
  A because the police could not protect people.
  B before any others in the country.
  C after 50,000 burglaries in the area.
  D because some residents wanted to go away for a holiday.

2 When members of a 'Watch' group see suspicious individuals, they
  A try and frighten them away.
  B contact the police.
  C try and arrest them.
  D call the other members of the 'Watch' group.

3 When a new 'Watch' scheme starts in an area,
  A people fit new locks to their doors and windows.
  B the police send fewer officers to the area.
  C burglars are less likely to break into houses.
  D residents put signs on their doors.

4 One other benefit of 'Watch' schemes is that
  A people get to know each other better.
  B members of the 'Watch' look after old people.
  C different kinds of people are attracted to live in the area.
  D old people are no longer frightened of crime.

5 In general, the author seems to think that
  A the police should do more to protect people.
  B 'Watch' schemes are not very useful in reducing crime.
  C the 'Neighbourhood Watch' schemes have been successful.
  D it is hard to have any privacy in a 'Neighbourhood Watch' area.

B Vocabulary 1

Find a word or phrase in the text which means:

1 strange, not quite right ________
2 carefully and without people noticing ________
3 people who live in a place ________
4 something which stops you doing something ________
5 people who destroy or damage things for no reason ________
6 watching carefully for something ________

C Language study 1

Rewrite these requests for permission using the word in bold. Pay particular attention to the tenses you use after *if*.

1 Could I stay for a few days?

stayed

Would it be ________________ for a few days?

2 Would you mind if I turned on the TV?

may

Excuse me, but ________________ on the TV?

3 Can I make a cup of tea?

mind

Do ________________ a cup of tea?

4 Could I have a bath now?

mind

Would you ________________ a bath now?

5 Do you mind me phoning my brother?

if

Is it ________________ my brother?

6 Would it be possible for me to take the car?

OK

Would it be ________________ the car?

7 Could I invite a few friends over?

mind

Would ________________ a friends over?

8 Can you take photographs in the museum?

allowed

Are ________________ in the museum?

D Language study 2

Match the questions A–F with the answers 1–6.

Example:

A <u>3</u> B __ C __ D __ E __ F __

A *Would it be OK if I did my homework in the dining room?*
B Would you mind if I made a cup of tea?
C Do you mind if I come back late this evening?
D Is it OK if my parents phone me here?
E Do you mind if I smoke?
F Would you mind if I had a bath now?

1 No, not at all. I'll give you a spare key.
2 Yes of course. Have they got the number?
3 *Yes, that would be fine as long as you clear everything away before dinner.*
4 No, not at all. There should be plenty of hot water.
5 Yes, I do. I find the smell quite disgusting.
6 No, help yourself. The kettle's just boiled.

E Language study 3

Report these commands and requests using *ask if, ask ... (not) to, tell ... to, tell ... not to.*

Examples:

'Please sit down.'	*He asked me to sit down.*
'Can I sit down?'	*He asked if he could sit down.*
'Sit down.'	*He told me to sit down.*
'Don't sit down.'	*He told me not to sit down.*

1 'May I open the window?' the boy asked.

____

2 'Look in the mirror before stopping,' the driving instructor said to me.

____

3 'Please don't tell anyone the news,' Janet said to her sister.

____

4 'Don't drive so fast!' Henry said to his wife.

____

5 'Would it be all right if I had the day off?' Laura asked her boss.

____

6 'May I borrow your tennis racket?' I asked John.

____

7 'Turn the music down,' Tim said to his son.

____

8 'Could you put the plates in the dishwasher, please?' Mrs Robinson asked Justin.

____

F Language study 4

Report these questions using the word in bold.

1 'Do you like animals?' Gary asked Laura.

if

Gary ________________ animals.

2 'When did you move in?' he asked her.

when

He asked ________________ in.

3 'Would you like a cup of tea?' she asked him.

he

She asked him ________________ a cup of tea.

4 'What have you come to talk about?' she asked him.

had

She asked him ________________ talk about.

5 'Will you be around on Saturday?' she asked him.

would

She asked him ________________ on Saturday.

6 'What are you going to do about it?' he asked her.

was

He asked her ________________ do about it.

7 'Are you going to go to the police?' she asked him.

if

She asked him ________________ go to the police.

8 'Where do you keep your dog?' she asked him.

his

She asked ________________ dog.

G Vocabulary 2

Look at the wordsquare. Can you find the things connected with houses? All the words go from left to right or top to bottom.

3 things you would find in a bathroom:

toilet, ____________, ____________

3 things connected with lighting and heating:

____________, ____________, ____________

3 types of house:

____________, ____________, ____________

3 rooms in a house:

____________, ____________, ____________

3 things you would find in the kitchen:

____________, ____________, ____________

R	B	U	N	G	A	L	O	W	R
W	E	F	D	S	T	K	V	D	A
S	D	V	C	F	T	I	E	V	D
H	R	G	H	R	I	T	N	D	I
S	O	C	A	E	C	C	L	S	A
T	**O**	**I**	**L**	**E**	**T**	H	A	H	T
C	M	B	E	Z	S	E	M	O	O
F	L	A	T	E	D	N	P	W	R
W	W	T	F	R	I	D	G	E	F
A	S	H	B	O	I	L	E	R	D

H Vocabulary 3

You might need some of the services that these people offer for your house. Look at the situations below and decide who you would call.

architect	electrician	locksmith	plumber
baby-sitter	glazier	decorator	carpenter

1 A radiator is leaking. ________

2 You want to make a new bedroom in the attic. ________

3 You need some new cupboards in the kitchen. ________

4 The paint is coming off the walls in the bathroom. ________

5 You are afraid that burglars might break into the house. ________

6 All the lights have suddenly gone out. ________

7 Someone has kicked a football through the window. ________

8 You've been invited out for dinner, but have a three-year-old child to look after. ________

I Vocabulary 4

What are the missing verbs or prepositions in the sentences? Write the answers in the wordcomb and find the name of something that might be important to you!

1 When Maisie was exactly 100 years old, the Queen sent her a telegram to ______ her on her birthday. (12)

2 In my dream, everyone was laughing ______ me. (2)

3 You really ______ me of my brother. You look like him and you sound just like him too. (6)

4 Maisie's neighbours rang the police to complain ______ the terrible noise the dogs were making. (5)

5 The judge made a special order to prevent Mrs Lovell ______ keeping animals again. (4)

6 No, I won't come out with you tonight. I'm not very interested ______ ballet. (2)

7 We might have a picnic tomorrow or we might not. It all ______ on the weather. (7)

8 As she didn't know the town, she asked the bus conductor to tell her where to ______ off. (3)

9 She ______ in passing her driving test at the third attempt. (9)

10 Mrs Hannay paid the baby-sitter £10 ______ looking after the children that evening. (3)

11 Our dog is very ______ at doing tricks! He ought to be on TV. (6)

12 She got top marks in all her exams, so her parents were very ______ with her. (7)

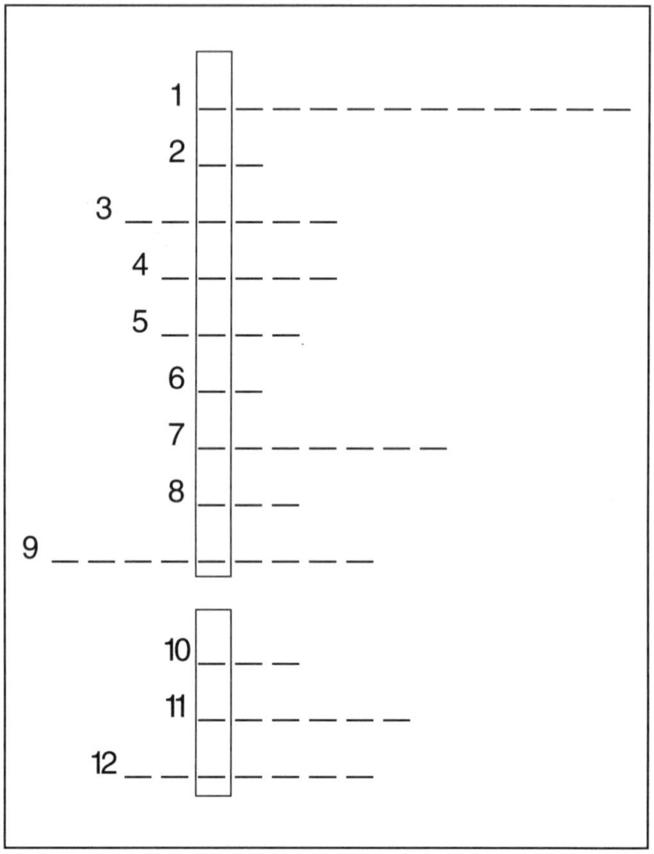

J Use of English

Complete the text with one word in each space. There is an example at the beginning (0).

AN ELDERLY couple (0)*who* were accused (1)________ carrying out a six-year campaign against their next-door neighbours, which included throwing dead chickens at their house, were fined a total (2)________ £6,000 yesterday. According (3)________ the prosecution, Brian Zipfell, 60, and Phyllis Hird, 71, attacked the next-door family in some way almost every day.

John and Pauline Barlow moved to their four-bedroom, detached house with their two children in 1990, but the move turned (4)________ to be far more difficult than they had expected. They were regularly insulted and sworn at by the elderly couple. As well (5)________ the chickens, they had snowballs, stones, coal, 80 wine corks and other missiles thrown at them. Whenever friends came to (6)________ on them, loud music would start next door. John Barlow asked the elderly couple (7)________ leave them alone and warned them that he (8)________ go to the police if they did not give (9)________ their campaign, but the problems continued.

The judge told Zipfell and Hird: 'Over a long period you both carried out a psychological campaign against your neighbours. I do not believe (10)________ allowing people to get away with this sort of thing, and this case calls (11)________ serious punishment. You and everyone else must be made to realize that we will not (12)________ up with this sort of behaviour between neighbours.'

Zipfell sat at the back of court in a wheelchair next to Hird during the hearing. (13)________ of them deny ever swearing at the Barlows (14)________ harassing them. However, Judge Fox found them guilty and fined them £6,000. He also ordered Hird to see a psychiatrist, saying he believed that she was mainly responsible (15)________ the attacks.

PROGRESS TEST 1

A Vocabulary cloze

Decide which word, A, B, C or D best fits each space. There is an example at the beginning (0).

HOPES AND DREAMS

Some years ago, my daughter was studying English at a university on the south coast. One evening she phoned to (0) *tell* me that what she really wanted to do was (1)_____ round the world, so she was looking (2)_____ the possibility of working in another country. She had seen several (3)_____ in the newspaper for student teachers of English abroad, and she was (4)_____ in one in Italy, which she was desperate to visit. She decided that this would be a good (5)_____ to achieve her ambition, so she was writing to (6)_____ for the job. The reply (7)_____ a long time to arrive, but eventually she received a letter asking if she (8)_____ go for an interview in London the following week. She was so excited that she immediately (9)_____ in touch with the school owner and agreed to attend the interview. She was determined that nothing would prevent her (10)_____ doing what she had set out to do. A (11)_____ days before the interview she had a very strange dream in which she (12)_____ birth to a beautiful baby. She was a little nervous and (13)_____ about the dream and phoned to ask me what I thought it might (14)_____ . As I knew something about dreams, I was able to assure her that it only symbolized her (15)_____ to do well in the interview.

0	A say	B talk
	C tell	D speak
1	A journey	B travel
	C voyage	D trip
2	A up	B over
	C into	D round
3	A notices	B posters
	C advertisements	D announcements
4	A interested	B keen
	C attracted	D enthusiastic
5	A path	B route
	C manner	D way
6	A claim	B inquire
	C request	D apply
7	A was	B took
	C spent	D passed
8	A should	B would
	C must	D will
9	A got	B came
	C went	D became
10	A of	B from
	C in	D about
11	A some	B several
	C few	D little
12	A made	B had
	C gave	D produced
13	A bored	B worried
	C offended	D annoyed
14	A intend	B mean
	C interpret	D realize
15	A desire	B request
	C want	D demand

B Open cloze

Think of ONE word which best fits each space. There is an example at the beginning (0).

AN ENVIABLE CAREER

Henry Adams is probably the luckiest person I know. I normally envy very (0) *few* of my friends' jobs because I am happy with what I do, but Henry Adams is one of those rare people (1)_______ job I would really like to have myself. Henry, (2)_______ had always been interested (3)_______ both science and animals, wanted to be a vet, and we were both students (4)_______ university at the same time.

When his course finished, (5)_______ went to Aberdeen, where he looked (6)_______ domestic animals (7)_______ as cats and dogs. He always said that he would like to move around because he didn't believe (8)_______ staying in any job for too long. So I wasn't very surprised when he gave (9)_______ that job and went to work in a zoo. He stayed there for two years, and in the evenings he studied hard to get some higher qualifications. When he had succeeded (10)_______ passing all his exams, he applied for a job (11)_______ a warden on a game reserve in Africa (12)_______ 1994. He is now responsible (13)_______ the well-being of thousands of animals. In addition, he is in charge (14)_______ a special programme to protect species (15)_______ are in danger of extinction.

C Key word transformations

Rewrite the sentences using the word in bold.

1 'Can I bring a friend to the party?' Jane wanted to know.

asked

Jane ________________ a friend to the party.

2 Simon gave up cigarettes when he was thirty.

stopped

Simon ________________ when he was thirty.

3 Few people speak Gaelic in Ireland.

many

There ________________ speak Gaelic in Ireland.

4 Running a big car like that can't be cheap.

must

It ________________ a big car like that.

5 Jennifer started teaching six years ago.

for

Jennifer ________________ six years.

6 'Could you please close the window?' the teacher asked Paul.

mind

The teacher asked Paul ________________ the window.

7 Tell me where you found this box of old books.

come

Where ________________ this box of old books?

8 I'd rather go to the cinema than watch TV tonight.

instead

Let's go to the cinema ________________ TV tonight.

9 'Don't shoot!' said the captain to his soldiers.

ordered

The captain ________________ shoot.

10 There was too much information for me to understand everything at once.

take

I wasn't ________________ all the information at once.

D Word formation

Complete the text with the correct form of the words in capitals. There is an example at the beginning (0).

NOT SUCH GOOD NEIGHBOURS

The families in our street are slowly being driven mad by the (0) *refusal* of the inhabitants of No.13 to have any form of (1)__________ with them. The trouble started over what is known as noise (2)__________ . Every evening, the (3)__________ neighbours used to turn up the volume on the TV so loud that no one in the (4)__________ was able to hear anything else. Not knowing what (5)__________ to take, local residents held a meeting to see if anyone had any (6)__________ as to how to deal with the problem. A (7)__________ was made to send a number of people to talk to the family in No.13 and ask them (8)__________ to turn their music down after six in the evening. Unfortunately the visit did not turn out to be (9)__________, as the inhabitants of No.13 refused to talk to them. So, on the (10)__________ of local police, the matter is now in the hands of the court.

0 REFUSE
1 COMMUNICATE
2 POLLUTE
3 THINK
4 NEIGHBOUR
5 ACT
6 SUGGEST
7 DECIDE
8 POLITE
9 SUCCESS
10 ADVISE

UNIT 6

A The Honesty Questionnaire

Read the questionnaire and answer the questions as honestly as you can. Then work out your score and see what it tells you about yourself.

1 You are spending the weekend at a friend's house. While you are doing the washing up, you accidentally crack what was clearly an expensive wine glass. Would you:
A hide the glass in the dustbin and hope that no one noticed?
B explain what had happened and perhaps offer to buy a new one?
C put the glass in the cupboard and not mention it?
D say that someone else had broken it?

2 You are with a small group of people on holiday. Someone expresses some strong political views on a subject, which you disagree with violently. Would you:
A say that you thought they were right?
B tell them quite bluntly that you thought they were talking rubbish?
C suggest tactfully that there were other ways of looking at the question?
D try and change the subject?

3 You are a member of a team playing a tennis match. At an important point in the game, your opponent hits the ball, which lands very near the line, and he/she asks you if the ball was in. You saw clearly that it was. Would you:
A play fair and say that the ball was in and give your opponent the point?
B cheat and say the ball was out and take the point yourself?
C say it would be best to play the point again?
D say you were not sure?

4 You and your boyfriend/girlfriend have been invited to a party, but you know your partner doesn't really want to go. You want to go because you know that someone you are very attracted to will be there. Would you:
A try and discourage your partner from going with you?
B be open and tell your partner why you really want to go?
C not go to the party at all?
D leave your partner to decide by himself/herself whether or not to go with you?

5 You work in a dress shop and you get paid commission on the dresses you sell. A woman is interested in a dress which does not suit her and asks you what you think of it. Would you:
A say it looks lovely but that you have seen something that might look even nicer?
B say only that you have seen another dress that might suit her more?
C tell her bluntly that it doesn't suit her?
D tell her that it looks very nice and is an excellent choice?

6 You have just found out that the boyfriend/girlfriend of a very close friend of yours has been seeing someone else. Your friend, who suspects something, asks if you know anything. Would you:
A beat about the bush and say that you weren't sure either way?
B be frank and tell them what you have heard?
C deny that you know anything?
D suggest that he/she should talk to their partner about it because it might be true?

7 You are selling your car because it has been very unreliable and has been very difficult to start, especially in the mornings. Someone from a town a long way away wants to buy it and has just asked you if it is reliable when starting. Would you:
A say that you have never had any serious problems with it?
B say that you are selling it because it is so bad at starting?
C try and cheat them by saying that it was particularly good at starting?
D say that it has been giving a bit of trouble recently but that the problem can be fixed easily?

8 Some people you know but find a bit boring have invited you to dinner at their house. Would you:
A say that you didn't want to go and why?
B accept and say that you were looking forward to it?
C say that you couldn't go because you were going to be busy?
D say you'd love to go, and then not turn up?

9 A friend of yours at school took a teacher's motorbike for fun, but had a crash and damaged the bike before returning it. The teacher has just asked you if you know anything about it. Would you:
A tell the teacher you think somebody completely different did it?
B say you know nothing about it?
C tell the teacher that your friend was responsible?
D tell a white lie and then try and persuade your friend to tell the teacher himself?

10 Someone you know has had her hair done. She looks awful, but the haircut cost a lot of money. Would you:
A not mention her haircut at all?
B tell her it suits her wonderfully?
C say it will take time to get used to it?
D ask her if she has had a fight with a hair dryer?

Now use the table below to add up your points, and see how honest you are.

1	A-2	B-4	C-3	D-1	6	A-2	B-4	C-1	D-3
2	A-1	B-4	C-3	D-2	7	A-2	B-4	C-1	D-3
3	A-4	B-1	C-3	D-2	8	A-4	B-2	C-3	D-1
4	A-1	B-4	C-3	D-2	9	A-1	B-2	C-4	D-3
5	A-2	B-3	C-4	D-1	10	A-2	B-1	C-3	D-4

Score:

10–16 You are not really the sort of person who would make a good friend. You lie, cheat and deceive people (including yourself) all the time. At times your dishonesty could almost be criminal. You had better learn to tell the truth, because you will never have any real friends if you carry on like this.

17–27 You don't tell the truth all the time, do you? You perhaps try to tell yourself that you lie to protect other people's feelings, but there is a little more to it than that. You are secretive, unreliable and a little untrustworthy. Try and be a little more open with your friends and the people you love, and don't try and avoid serious problems by lying.

28–35 You would be a good person to have as a friend. You can be trusted and don't delight in making people feel bad for no reason. You are the sort of person who can keep a promise and you don't run away from problems that need to be talked about. The only real lies you would tell are white lies as you are tactful and caring.

36–40 You must be very difficult to live with. You say exactly what you think. You like to think you are straight and honest, but you are often very blunt and rude, and hurt people's feelings for no reason. You are extremely open, and when someone asks you for an opinion, they know they will get the truth. But are you sure that the absolute truth is really what they always want to hear?

B Vocabulary 1

Choose a word or phrase from the questionnaire that means the opposite of the word or phrase in the table below. There is an example at the beginning (0).

honesty	0 *dis*honesty
1 _____	tactlessly
2 _____	to cheat
3 _____	to be secretive
reliable	4 _____
to tell the truth	5 _____
6 _____	to break a promise

C Language study 1

Rewrite these sentences using *wish* and *if only*. Use the word in bold.

Example:

I'm so tired of listening to your complaints.

would

I *wish you would stop* complaining.

1 It's such a shame Peter isn't here.
wish
I ________________ here.

2 I hate having so few friends.
only
If ________________ friends.

3 I would be so happy if the weather was warmer.
wish
I ________________ warmer.

4 It's such a shame we can't be friends.
only
If ________________ friends.

5 Do you ever regret not being famous?
wish
Do you ________________ famous?

6 It's such a pity I'm so bad at maths.
better
If ________________ maths.

D Use of English 1

Read these descriptions of two TV programmes. Decide which word, A, B, C or D, best fits each space. There is an example at the beginning (0).

Film: *Wall Street* (C4, 10.25 p.m.)

'Greed is good,' (0) *says* Gecko (Michael Douglas), a 1980s businessman who (1)_____ a fortune from buying companies and selling them off. He (2)_____ together with an ambitious youngster (Charlie Sheen) and (3)_____ out a plan for an even bigger take-over. However, it (4)_____ out that the young man's father will (5)_____ his job if Gecko (6)_____ to bring the deal (7)_____ . The action (8)_____ place in New York, where the director's father was a broker, and the bitter view seems to be based on personal experience.
(Dir. Oliver Stone, 1987)

Film: *Abandoned* (BBC1, 11.15 p.m.)

This tense TV thriller tells the (9)_____ of Mary Bligh (Elizabeth Dow), who (10)_____ money from a London gang so that she can feed her family. When they realize that she will never be able to (11)_____ back the money they have (12)_____ her, they force her to take part in their (13)_____ activities. She runs away and several members of her family are killed. When she later (14)_____ a fortune on the Lottery, she returns to take (15)_____ on the criminals.
(Dir. Harry Benson, 1996)

0	A tells	B says	C speaks	D talks
1	A pays	B earns	C deals	D does
2	A works	B meets	C comes	D gets
3	A works	B takes	C puts	D makes
4	A turns	B comes	C ends	D happens
5	A sack	B fire	C miss	D lose
6	A realizes	B succeeds	C achieves	D manages
7	A off	B up	C over	D out
8	A takes	B has	C holds	D finds
9	A plot	B events	C story	D plan
10	A borrows	B lends	C gains	D pays
11	A pay	B buy	C lend	D owe
12	A lent	B borrowed	C owed	D bought
13	A thief	B crook	C criminal	D gangster
14	A gains	B wins	C earns	D has
15	A attack	B revenge	C repayment	D return

E Language study 2

Complete the letter from a TV viewer to the programme *Viewpoint*. Use the correct form of the words in capitals. There is an example at the beginning (0).

Dear Viewpoint,

I am becoming increasingly (0) *worried* about the quality of programmes on television. I have therefore decided to write to say how (1)__________ I am that you cannot think of anything more (2)__________ to offer the public.

I was very (3)__________ to hear that you are planning to show even more police dramas, which many people find very (4)__________, and I doubt whether any viewers will be (5)__________ by your new (and probably very (6)__________) hospital drama series.

A few years ago, there were far more (7)__________ documentaries and (8)__________ films on TV, but everything seems to have changed. I find it (9)__________ that your standards have fallen so low, but, sadly, I am not (10)__________ that things will improve.

0 WORRY
1 DISAPPOINT
2 INTEREST
3 ANNOY
4 BORE
5 AMUSE
6 DEPRESS
7 FASCINATE
8 EXCITE
9 ASTONISH
10 CONVINCE

F Language study 3

Look at these situations and imagine what each person might say, using *I wish ...*.

> ***Remember:*** use *would(n't)* when you are complaining about someone els's behaviour, but do not say: *I wish I would ...*

Examples:

Jenny's son has a lot of annoying habits.
I wish he wouldn't make such a mess.

Anna told her horrible boss exactly what she thought of him yesterday, and now she is worried.
I wish I hadn't been so rude to him.

1 Jenny's son is complaining about his mother.

____

2 George sold his shares a few weeks ago for 235p and now they have gone up to 894p.

____

3 Jason is fed up with the behaviour of Sam, one of the other students in his class.

____

4 Lars has just started his military service, and doesn't like they way they treat him.

____

5 Mick is in prison.

____

6 Harry has just split up with his girlfriend because she was unhappy with the way he behaved.

____

7 Peter went for a drive and is now completely lost.

____

8 Mrs Green's children have left home, and they rarely get in touch with her.

____

G Use of English 2

Rewrite these sentences using the word in bold.

1 I didn't find his jokes at all amusing.
by
I was ________________ his jokes.

2 He regrets resigning, because he can't find a job.
wishes
He ________________ because he can't find a job.

3 Could I borrow your bike this afternoon?
lend
Could ________________ this afternoon?

4 I hate the way you treat my mother.
wish
I ________________ my mother like that.

5 I wasn't frightened by the film, but my sister was terrified.
find
I didn't ________________, but my sister was terrified.

6 It's such a pity I lost her phone number.
only
If ________________ her phone number.

H Vocabulary 2

Find the missing adjectives or prepositions and write them in the squares. Look for words like *responsible for* and *proud of*. The number in brackets at the end of each clue tells you how long the word is.

ACROSS

1 I'm not surprised that he forgot your birthday. It's absolutely typical _____ him. (2)
3 The gunman should not be approached. He is highly dangerous and is _____ of doing almost anything – including shooting. (7)
7 You behaved very badly at the party. Even I was quite shocked _____ some of the things you said. (2)
8 Jan passed all her exams with good grades, so she was very _____ with her results. (7)
9 I think I'm going to try and get a new job. I'm fed _____ with the way my boss shouts at me. (2)
10 Jane's terribly_____ about what has happened to her cat. It hasn't been home for three days. (7)
11 I've always needed a calculator, because I'm not exactly brilliant _____ maths. (2)
13 She suffers from claustrophobia – that means she's _____ of enclosed spaces. (6)
16 You really needn't have bought me a present, but it's very _____ of you all the same. (4)
17 I was always terrible _____ tennis because I've got such bad eyesight. (2)
18 I find languages very difficult to learn, but I'm quite _____ at science. (4)
20 The opposite of *yes*. (2)
22 I feel very _____ for George. He has had such an unhappy life. (5)
23 My teacher was very pleased _____ me because I got all the answers right. (4)

DOWN

2 You'll have to type this letter again, I'm afraid. It's _____ _____ spelling mistakes. (4,2)
3 How did you manage to do such a difficult sum so quickly? It was very _____ of you. (6)
4 Why was he shouting at you? What was he so angry _____? (5)
5 She's crying because she's upset _____ some of the things you said. (2)
6 The children are really _____ about their holiday in Disneyland next week. (7)
12 She's very fond _____ her nephew. (2)
13 She's very quick _____ running. (2)
14 You shouldn't have started eating before they sat down. It was very _____ _____ you. (4,2)
15 I've never been interested _____ politics. (2)
16 She's very _____ on gardening. In fact, she spends most of her free time doing it. (4)
17 The contract is fine, on the whole, but there are one or two things I'm not happy _____. (5)
19 I've interviewed a few people but so far there's been no one I've been very impressed _____. (2)
21 I like tennis a lot, but I'm not all that keen _____ squash. (2)

UNIT 7

A Reading

Read this article written by a seventeen-year-old about how people react to your problems and choose the best answer in 1–7.

Get a Grip on Yourself

How many times have you heard those words?

You've got a problem, right? So you carry it around with you for a while until it gets too bad to keep to yourself. So you screw up your courage and find someone to talk to about it. And every time, the conversation finishes something like this, 'You've just got to get a grip on yourself, Paula.'

Ask me, how do I feel after that? I'll tell you. I feel stupid, inadequate and actually very angry. You see, what I really wanted was some advice ...

Let me tell you something about the sort of people who tell you to get a grip on yourself. There are two types, basically. Firstly, there are the busy-bees. You know that they don't want to listen to your problems and that they find it very embarrassing anyway.

Worse, though, are the people who seem to be only too willing to listen. You pour out your heart and are about to cry on their shoulder when they put on that special voice and suddenly say, 'Get a grip on yourself.'

Telling yourself to get a grip simply doesn't work. You've tried to think things through, but it's so difficult and you get stuck somewhere in the middle, unable to go on. So you try to behave as if nothing has happened, and you end up in an even bigger mess.

The trouble is that the Get-a-grip types really believe that they've given you the best advice possible. In fact, it's only a thinly-disguised criticism, telling you to stop wasting their time and accept the blame for whatever's gone wrong. They think they're being helpful but, the truth is, they just don't want to know.

If you want my advice, when you hear those words, stop right there and say, 'Thank you, but no thank you.'

1 According to Paula, what do most people eventually do when they have a difficult problem to solve?
   A Keep it to themselves.
   B Pretend that it doesn't exist.
   C Ask people they know for advice.
   D Cry on someone's shoulder.

2 'Get a grip on yourself' (GAGOY) are words which
   A the writer hardly ever hears.
   B are used by angry, stupid and inadequate people.
   C cause more problems than they solve.
   D help people to cope with their problems.

3 The first category of people who use GAGOY are those who
   A feel sympathy for you but can't express it.
   B have no real interest in the problems of others.
   C can't wait to hear more about your problems.
   D cause you intense discomfort.

4 The second category of GAGOY users are those who
   A offer a sensible solution to your problem.
   B gently encourage you to forget about your problem.
   C while appearing sympathetic are similar to those in the first category.
   D listen sympathetically then say nothing at all.

5 The worst thing about GAGOY users is that they
   A pretend that nothing is your fault.
   B tell you that you are wasting their time.
   C pretend they aren't interested in you at all.
   D believe that they have given you good advice.

6 Paula suggests that if you hear the words 'Get a grip on yourself', you should
   A break off your conversation immediately and escape.
   B turn to professional helpers for advice.
   C avoid looking at the person saying the words.
   D pretend your problem doesn't exist.

7 What do we learn about Paula from reading the article?
   A She never talks to anybody about her real problems.
   B She gets angry when people give her some advice.
   C She dislikes people who expect you to cope with your problems.
   D She respects people who will willingly listen to your problems.

B Language study 1

a *If you mix the colours yellow and green, you get brown.*
b *If I can afford it, we'll go and have a pizza.*
c *If I were taller, I would join the police force.*

Which sentence suggests that something might happen?
Which sentence is highly improbable?
Which sentence tells you that something is always true?

Complete the following sentences with the correct form of the verb in brackets and state which type of conditional sentence (a, b or c) you have made.

1 If they arrive in time, we ________ (go) to the cinema.
2 If you ________ (smoke) you risk damaging your health.
3 If you put water in a freezer, it ________ (turn) to ice.
4 If we ________ (get) stuck in a traffic jam, we'll miss the plane.
5 If I were rich, I ________ (give) a lot of money to charity.
6 If he ________ (not be) so untidy, he would be a perfect husband!
7 If your dog chases my cat any more, I ________ (report) you to the police!
8 If you could live anywhere in the world, where ________ (you/choose)?

C Vocabulary

Choose one of the words below in its correct form to complete the sentences. More than one answer may be possible.

fault error mistake blame defect

1 I think you've made a(n) ________ . I'm not John, I'm his brother!
2 Don't ________ me for what happened. It wasn't my ________ .
3 The telephone bill was sent to you in ________ .
4 There are some ________ in the design of this computer.
5 You've made the same ________ six times in this homework.
6 The children always get the ________ for everything that goes wrong!

D Use of English 1

Read Stephen's letter to Peter. If a line is correct, put a tick (✓). If a line has an unnecessary word, underline it. There are two examples at the beginning (0) and (00).

Dear Peter,
0 Well, here we are at last! We'd been looking forward to ✓
00 coming back for the ages and we finally arrived safe and
1 sound for last week. Since then we've been trying to
2 organize the flat and find schools for the children. We've
3 had to borrow off some furniture from friends and relatives
4 as the flat we're renting got turned out to be unfurnished!
5 Sally says that it's all by our own fault. We should have
6 checked the details more carefully! I thought it seemed a
7 good value for money! It was difficult to make it the
8 decision to come home as we had been living and working in
9 abroad for so long. I think we're going to find it strange
10 to settle down here again. I haven't started looking for
11 a job yet as I've been so busy. I'll give you a call so to
12 arrange a night when you can come to dinner and we can
13 discuss about old times! Looking forward to seeing you again.
Best wishes, Stephen

E Use of English 2

Read the letter to an advice column and the reply it received. Think of ONE word which best fits each space. There is an example at the beginning (0).

Dear Margaret,

Please can you tell me how (0) *to* stop smoking? My girl-friend and I have split (1)________ and it's all (2)________ fault because she says she can't stand my smoking (3)________ longer. If I (4)________ able to stop smoking, she says she will go out with me again.

'Desperate',
London

Dear 'Desperate' of London,

Here is (5)________ useful advice which might help you to solve your problem. First, think (6)________ where and when you usually have a cigarette. If you really want to succeed in giving (7)________ smoking, these times and places are going to be danger spots, so try and avoid them.

Next, choose a day (8)________ you are not under too much stress to stop. On that day, tell (9)________ how much healthier you will be if you can succeed. Make sure that you replace your cigarettes (10)________ something just for you – a special treat!

Many people have tried several times to do the (11)________ thing. If you have failed once or twice, ask yourself, 'Why (12)________ I start again?' This might help you to succeed the (13)________ time you try. Remember – every day (14)________ a cigarette is a triumph. And, you might succeed (15)________ getting your girl-friend back!

F Language study 2

Rewrite the reported conversation below in direct speech using the exact words of each speaker. The beginning has been done for you.

The police officer asked Tom where he had been on the night of the robbery. Tom replied that he had been out for the evening with some friends. P.C. Dent went on to ask Tom what they had been doing and Tom told him that they had been to see a film and then had gone to a nearby pub for a drink.

P.C. Dent then wanted to know what time Tom had arrived home, but Tom couldn't remember exactly.

The police officer enquired whether any of the neighbours might have heard Tom coming home, but Tom was sure that they hadn't because he had been very quiet. He hadn't wanted to wake up his father, who had to get up very early in the morning to go to work.

Tom apologised for not being able to prove his story since his friends had all gone away on holiday.

P.C. Dent: *Where were you on the night of the robbery?*

Tom: *I was out for the evening with some friends.*

G Language study 3

Here is the rest of the conversation between Tom and the police officer. Report what they said to each other. The beginning has been done for you. These phrases will help you:

promise to do something
threaten to do something
suggest (to someone) that they should
promise (someone) that
tell someone (to)
order someone to
insist that

P.C. Dent: Tom, you're just not telling the truth!

Tom: What about talking to the owner of the pub? He'll remember me.

P.C. Dent: We've already done that and we've shown him your photograph, but he can't remember you at all.

Tom: Well, it was very busy that night. Perhaps he just didn't notice me.

P.C. Dent: Put your coat on, please, and come with me to the police station. We'll have to continue our enquiries there.

Tom: OK. I'll get my coat. I swear to you that I didn't do that robbery. If you send me to prison, I'll make life very difficult for you later.

The police officer insisted that Tom wasn't telling the truth.

H Language study 4

Complete the sentences with *still, already* and *yet* using one of the sentence types below.

a *You still haven't told me.*
b *You've already told me.*
c *You haven't told me yet.*

Example:
You promised you would lend me the book but you *still haven't lent it to me.*

> ***Remember:*** sentences *a* and *c* have almost the same meaning. But *a* is slightly stronger in meaning and more emphatic than *c*.

1 Could you please do your homework now because you ________________?

2 Please don't show me the letter again because you've ________________

3 We've been waiting for the tickets for two weeks but they ________________

4 Could I keep the book for another few days because I ________________?

5 I've asked him three times to lay the table but he ________________

6 I'm not going to write to him again. I ________________

I Writing

This letter appeared in an advice column. Read carefully the letter and the notes you have made. Then write a letter to J. R. Simmons suggesting three different solutions to the problem and saying which you think is the best one.

> *Dear Mary,*
>
> *The company I work for has given me the opportunity to go and work abroad for six months. Although I would really like to go, I live with my mother, who is not very well and relies on me to do many of the jobs around the house. Despite my assurance that our neighbours will keep an eye on her and help out in an emergency, she is still worried at the thought of being alone in the house all the time.*
>
> *What would you advise me to do?*
>
> *J. R. Simmons*
>
> Possible solutions:
>
> 1 employ live-in housekeeper?
>
> 2 take mother too?
>
> 3 put mother in nursing home?

Write a letter of 120–180 words in an appropriate style. Do not write any addresses.

UNIT 8

A Reading

Read the article in which a mother talks about her daughter and the effects of anorexia: a medical condition in which someone has no desire to eat anything at all. Eight sentences have been removed from the article. Choose from sentences A–I the one which fits each gap (1–7). There is one extra sentence which you do not need. There is an example at the beginning (0).

DON'T LET IT HAPPEN TO YOUR DAUGHTER

'The change in our daughter Jo was so gradual we didn't really take it too seriously to begin with,' admits Wendy, 42. 'Being on a diet seemed quite normal for a teenager. [0 *I*] She changed from a well-built, happy athletic girl of 16 into a pale, irritable walking skeleton. And the more we tried to get her to eat, the more she rebelled.'

'No one was allowed near her when she was eating. [1 ___] She also insisted on cooking for the rest of us. But we eventually gave up trying to get her to accept food from us.

[2 ___] She always seemed to be on the go – cooking, clearing the table – often before the rest of us had even finished – and washing up. For a long time she refused to even believe she had a problem. [3 ___]'

'Eventually she was so weak I got her admitted into hospital with the doctor's help. My husband and I had to literally drag her screaming into the car. [4 ___] Jo was gripped with fear and panic and I felt so guilty. But we were desperate. We thought that in hospital she might discover that she actually did not want to break free of her condition.'

'[5 ___] The doctor told us that the best thing we could do was to leave. At this point Jo started to sob uncontrollably. 'Don't leave me, Mummy,' she begged. 'Please don't leave me.'

[6 ___] They got her strength up by feeding her and then arranged for her to see the hospital psychiatrist, who recommended her for specialist help.'

'Jo's recovery has been slow. Living with her is like living on a knife edge where the slightest word can trigger sobbing and screaming and wild accusations. At first I just felt this terrible guilt. [7 ___] I don't think Jo will ever be free of her anorexia but she is learning to keep it under control.'

A That dreadful moment will stay in my mind for ever.

B Turning my back on her cries and leaving her there was the hardest thing I'd ever had to do.

C But afterwards I felt this terrible frustration at not being able to help her.

D Teenagers, in my opinion, usually have huge appetites.

E When we got there she'd calmed down into an angry silence.

F Any attempt was met with screaming and hysterical fits.

G She'd shut herself in the kitchen and then sneak up to her bedroom which always remained locked, and strictly out of bounds.

H During this time all we could do was watch while our daughter slowly starved herself to death.

I But her slimming got out of control.

B Vocabulary

Match the words and phrases on the left with the meanings on the right.

Example: 1d

1 irritable	a) in a tricky or dangerous situation
2 frustration	b) awful or terrible
3 dreadful	c) fought back
4 on the go	d) angry or bad-tempered
5 trigger	e) disappointment or dissatisfaction
6 drag	f) seized by
7 sneak	g) pull
8 gripped with	h) cause to happen
9 rebelled	i) busy
10 on a knife edge	j) slip away without being noticed

C Language study 1

Rewrite the sentences using *just about to (do), was just (doing),* or *had just (done).*

Example:
Sheila had one foot in the bathwater when the telephone rang.
Sheila *was just about to have a bath when the telephone rang.*

1 Sheila was in the bath when there was a knock at the door.

Sheila ______________________________

____

2 Ann had been on the point of ringing the bell. She noticed that the door was slightly open.

Ann ______________________________

____

3 Ann closed the door. Then she dropped her handbag.

Ann ______________________________

____

4 Sheila finished her bath. She heard a noise.

Sheila ______________________________

____

5 Ann picked up her handbag and at the same time she knocked over a chair.

Ann ______________________________

____

6 Sheila decided to phone the police. She heard another noise.

Sheila ______________________________

____

7 Ann called out to Sheila. She noticed Sheila standing by the phone.

Ann ______________________________

____

8 Sheila dialled 999, and at the same time she heard a familiar voice shouting her name.

Sheila ______________________________

____

9 She put down the phone. Then she saw her friend Ann standing in the doorway.

Sheila ______________________________

____

D Language study 2

Use the notes to make sentences of your own using either *so...that* or *such...that*.

Example: *film/boring*

so ______________

such ______________

The film was so boring that we walked out of the cinema.

It was such a boring film that we walked out of the cinema.

> ***Remember:*** *so* comes before an adjective (without nouns) and *such (a)* comes before a noun (with or without adjectives).

1 students/enthusiastic

so ______________________________

2 car/expensive

such ______________________________

3 rent/high

so ______________________________

4 city/crowded

such ______________________________

5 football players/good

so ______________________________

6 coffee/strong

so ______________________________

7 journey/long

such ______________________________

8 children/naughty

such ______________________________

9 company/successful

so ______________________________

10 film star/talented

such ______________________________

E Language study 3

Combine the words on the left and the sentences on the right to make sentences of your own with *too*.

Example:

4 cold	h I don't fancy going for a swim today.

It's too cold to go for a swim today.

1 exhausted	a We can't play tennis in this rain!
2 lazy	b Parents of young children hardly ever relax.
3 mean	c Susan can't reach the books on the top shelf.
4 cold	d David doesn't feel like doing his homework.
5 wet	e The baby can't speak yet.
6 short	f The children refuse to take any physical exercise.
7 young	g My sister never spends any money.
8 busy	h I don't fancy going for a swim today.

F Vocabulary 3

Five of these words may be used in combination with *ache*. Which ones are they? Tick (✓) the correct words.

tooth	arm	shoulder	back
leg	head	eye	hand
ear	stomach	elbow	wrist

G Use of English

Read the text and decide which word, A, B, C or D, best fits each space. There is an example at the beginning (0).

It was a Monday morning in the office and, as (0) <u>usual</u>, everyone was busy sorting through their mail before starting work. The other staff had (1)_____ that Nicky, one of the computer operators, had been (2)_____ rather miserable recently and they wondered what might have happened to make her so (3)_____ . Suddenly Nicky accidentally (4)_____ over a cup of coffee. As she was clearing up the mess, the girl sitting next to her happened to glance at Nicky's right hand. There was a large swelling at the (5)_____ . 'What on earth have you (6)_____ to yourself? Does it (7)_____?' asked the girl. 'Yes, it does. I think I've (8)_____ it using the computer,' replied Nicky. 'I think you'd better go and let the doctor (9)_____ it,' said the girl. 'Let's hope there's no permanent (10)_____ to your hand.'

	A	B	C	D
0	A normal	B everyday	C usual	D ordinary
1	A recognized	B realized	C noticed	D identified
2	A appearing	B seeming	C pretending	D looking
3	A sick	B bored	C uninterested	D depressed
4	A kicked	B punched	C hit	D knocked
5	A wrist	B elbow	C knee	D ankle
6	A made	B done	C happened	D brought
7	A harm	B hurt	C disturb	D upset
8	A injured	B ruined	C spoiled	D destroyed
9	A check	B inspect	C examine	D investigate
10	A pain	B destruction	C damage	D suffering

H Language study 4

Rewrite these sentences using the word in bold.

> ***Remember:*** we use *used to (do)* for something we often did in the past but not now. We use *be/get used to (doing)* when we accept something as normal routine.

1 I gave up smoking ten years ago.

used

I ________________ ten years ago.

2 When I was a teenager, I went to a lot of dances.

used

When I was a teenager, I ________________ to a lot of dances.

3 I hate living here but I'll probably like it more in time.

used

I hate living here but I'll probably ________________ it in time.

4 Hard work doesn't bother me.

used

I ________________ hard.

5 My brother quickly adapted to his new job at the bank.

used

My brother quickly ________________ his new job at the bank.

6 We had lots of friends when we lived in the country.

have

We ________________ lots of friends when we lived in the country.

7 Peter was so difficult as a child.

be

Peter ________________ so difficult as a child.

8 When you buy a new car, you need some time to practise driving it.

get

When you buy a new car, you need some time to ________________ driving it.

9 John is beginning to like living on his own.

getting

John ________________ living on his own.

10 I can't see myself ever being happy to live in a cold climate.

get

I'll never ________________ in a cold climate.

I Language study 5

The words in the sentences below have been put in the wrong order. Put them in the correct order.

Example:
skirt cotton yellow a little pretty
= *a pretty little yellow cotton skirt*

1 black new handbag a leather

____

2 square table huge wooden a

____

3 French small a cheese round

____

4 leather beautiful jacket green a

____

5 an bottle unusual Italian glass red

____

6 silk a dress blue Japanese long lovely

____

UNIT 9

A Reading

Read the text and choose the best answer in 1–6.

Western people rely on technical and mechanical solutions in everything they do. Refrigerators preserve their food, washing machines clean their underwear and computers are supposed to solve all their problems. When they are ill, they rely on the surgeon's knife. If their hearts are running down, then they must be repaired; if they cannot be repaired, they should be replaced, just as an old car sometimes gets a new engine. But up to now we have had a shortage of donors to give their hearts: to keep one person alive, another donor had to die.

Nowadays there is more and more talk about using monkeys. Every monkey has a near-human heart, and humans have always been over careful in respecting the lives and well-being of other animals. This includes the life and well-being of other humans. Therefore in the early years of the 21st century – I was told – the mass killings of monkeys may occur. We'll need to use their hearts for human consumption.

Monkeys, on the whole, are happier creatures than their near relatives, Homo Sapiens, or man. They know fear, of course, and they face real dangers, but they are also more intelligent than us. They create no unnecessary dangers for themselves; they run no businesses, chase no money, are unimpressed by gold – that utterly useless metal, and they do not care at all about hell or evil spirits. I have a vague feeling that it is not monkeys' hearts that we ought to implant in ourselves, but monkeys' brains.

1 According to the author, Westerners believe health problems can be solved by
   A spending more money on scientific research.
   B taking more precautions.
   C using technical or mechanical methods.
   D increasing the number of doctors.

2 The problem with heart transplants has been that
   A artificial hearts do not work very well.
   B there are not usually enough donors.
   C some of the heart donors are too old.
   D many people die after the operations.

3 The author suggests that in the future
   A people will care less about other human beings.
   B monkey hearts will form part of our diet.
   C monkeys will become extinct.
   D monkey hearts will be used in transplant operations.

4 The author says that monkeys
   A live in a relatively safe world in the jungle.
   B are not capable of feeling emotions like fear.
   C are not capable of logical thinking.
   D are usually more content than humans.

5 The author suggests that
   A human beings will return to a more natural lifestyle.
   B we are wrong to think of ourselves as cleverer than monkeys.
   C monkeys would be better at running the world than humans.
   D scientists should work out how to do brain transplants.

6 The main point the author is making is that humans
   A make life more complicated that it needs to be.
   B have no right to make use of other animals.
   C should worry less about growing old.
   D are similar in many ways to monkeys.

B Vocabulary 1

Find a word or phrase in the text which means:

1 prevent from decaying ________
2 losing power, working more slowly ________
3 a lack of, not enough of ________
4 not clear or definite ________
5 to put into a body ________

C Vocabulary 2

Read the text about smallpox. Then fill in the spaces in each section with one of the words from the box above it.

victim	symptoms	spread
disease	died	epidemics

For thousands of years, smallpox was a terrifying (1)________ which threatened people in every continent, and every few years there were (2)________ which killed millions of people. It is believed that the disease began in China and then (3)________ slowly to the other continents. The first known (4)________ was Rameses V, the pharaoh of Egypt, who showed all the main (5)________ of the disease, including the terrible rash, and who (6)________ of it in 1157 BC.

vaccinate	protect	serious
infected	cure	

Over the centuries, many doctors tried to find a (7)________ for the disease but none suceeded. However, in 1774, a doctor called Edward Jenner decided to investigate the belief that people who had had cowpox could not be (8)________ with smallpox. Cowpox was a much less (9)________ disease, and hardly ever caused any lasting problems. Jenner discovered that it was possible to (10)________ people from smallpox by giving them cowpox first, and he began to (11)________ large numbers of people against the disease.

treatment	virus	immune
eradicated	recovered	

It was soon clear that anyone who had had a vaccination was (12)________ to smallpox. This was because humans, when they are infected with cowpox, produce antibodies; these protect people by attacking and killing the smallpox (13)________ if it enters the body.

Vaccination has become the standard (14)________ for the disease, although no cure has ever been found. In 1958, the World Health Organisation decided to try and vaccinate everyone in the world, and after a massive international campaign, smallpox was (15)________.

The last man in the world to catch it was Ali Maow Maalin from Merka in Somalia – and fortunately he (16)________ from the disease.

D Language study 1

Fill in the spaces with the correct form of *make* or *let*. You may have to change the tenses. There are two examples at the beginning.

I hated doing National Service. The officers *made* me clean the toilets every morning.

Her parents are very strict with her. They never *let* her go out in the evenings.

1 I love his sense of humour – he always ________ me laugh.

2 I like our English teacher, but she ________ us work very hard.

3 My boss is very good to me – he ________ me have time off whenever I want.

4 Do you think your father would ________ you use the car if you asked him nicely?

5 I lost my key, but luckily my brother was in so he ________ me in.

6 If you eat too much chocolate, it will ________ you fat.

7 Her parents ________ her go to the party because they thought she was too young to go out by herself.

8 Please don't interrupt her. ________ her speak.

E Language study 2

Fill in the spaces in the sentences below with *although/even though* or *despite/in spite of*.

> ***Remember:*** *although* and *even though* are followed by a subject + verb. We use *despite* and *in spite of* with a noun or *-ing* form, or with *the fact that* + verb.

1 The doctor recognized her at once, ________ the fact that he hadn't seen her for several years.

2 ________ she said she didn't know very much about flowers, she had the most beautiful garden.

3 ________ having no formal medical qualifications, my acupuncturist has helped me a lot.

4 ________ never having learned Italian at school, he soon picked it up when he was in Florence.

5 The house felt terribly cold ________ the fact that the central heating had been on all day.

6 ________ she liked him a lot, she didn't want to marry him.

F Phrasal verbs

Rewrite these sentences using the word in bold.

1 The thief ran away when the police arrived.
cleared
The thief ________________ soon as the police arrived.

2 On her father's death, Anna took over the business.
passed
When ________________, Anna took over the business.

3 Ronald robbed a bank but wasn't caught, and went to live in South America.
away
Ronald robbed a bank but ________________ it, and went to live in South America.

4 Seeing Peter made her faint and fall to the floor.
passed
When she ________________ and fell to the floor.

5 The old lady trusted the con man completely, and lost all her savings.
took
The con man ________________ completely, and she lost all her savings.

6 You can go out when your bedroom is tidy.
cleared
You can go out as soon ________________ your bedroom.

7 The lorry driver hit and killed a cat in the road.
ran
The lorry driver ________________ a cat in the road.

8 We aren't going to employ any more people until the winter.
taking
We aren't ________________ until the winter.

G Use of English 1

Read the text. If a line is correct, put a tick (✓). If a line has an unnecessary word, underline it. There are two examples at the beginning (0) and (00).

0 The other day, when I was in London, I ran <u>down</u> into
00 an old friend of mine who had been at university ✓
1 with me. Although that we hadn't seen each other
2 for ages and had lost the touch, it was just like old
3 times, and he told me all his news.
4 He moved to London after leaving from university,
5 and started to train as an accountant. He left after
6 a few of months because he didn't find it very
7 interesting, and he didn't feel like it spending the
8 rest of his life in an office. His parents were very
9 helpful – they didn't try to make him to carry on
10 training as a chartered accountant, and said him
11 they would continue to support him despite of the
12 fact that he didn't have a job to go to. He soon found
13 work doing that what he really wanted – writing
14 for a TV show. After the first series end, the producer
15 let him to have his own TV show even though
he was relatively young, and it turned out to be a
great success.

H Vocabulary 3

Look through the following character adjectives and say whether they are:

A good qualities
B qualities that may be good or bad
C bad qualities

shy	mean	conceited
enthusiastic	faithful	reliable
predictable	frank	talkative
patient	tense	ambitious
generous	aggressive	considerate

Now use ten of the words to complete the following sentences.

Example:
Jack is very *enthusiastic* about going on holiday with us, and says he can't wait.

1 I always know exactly what my mother is going to say – she is so ___________ .
2 The driver was very ___________ . At the lights, he got out of his car and tried to hit me.
3 Jane is very ___________ . She will always tell you exactly what she thinks even if you won't like it.
4 He is a very ___________ politician. They say he wants to become prime minister one day.
5 Cathy hates going to parties because she's very ___________ and avoids talking to new people.
6 If Brian has promised to give you a lift to the airport, I can assure you he will come. He is very ___________ .

I Use of English 2

Read the text and decide which word, A, B, C or D, best fits each space. There is an example at the beginning (0).

BODY AND MIND

People have tried (0) *for* over 2000 years to find a relationship (1)_____ people's physical features and their character, and even (2)_____ there is a complete (3)_____ of evidence for such an idea, it is still popular.

The Ancient Greeks were interested in the idea of human personality (4)_____ they did not link it with outward appearance. Later, during the Renaissance, some writers (5)_____ that there was a direct connection between a person's character and their face, and they called this new science physiognomy. They thought that the new science would (6)_____ you know a great deal about a person simply by analysing their face. Kings and princes were (7)_____ in the science, as they thought it might (8)_____ them to be better judges of character, and they believed that these new skills would (9)_____ it more difficult for dishonest courtiers to (10)_____ them in.

(11)_____ the fact that nobody takes these theories seriously nowadays, scientists are still interested in the basic idea. They have shown that there is a link between a person's character and their build. Extroverts and other confident, (12)_____ people are usually short and thick set, and in contrast, people who are (13)_____ and reserved tend to be (14)_____ and thin. There is some scientific basis to this theory because glands have such an important effect on both a person's build and their moods, so it is not (15)_____ to find a link between them.

0	A for	B during	C in	D since
1	A between	B among	C from	D with
2	A still	B yet	C since	D though
3	A lack	B shortage	C failure	D need
4	A despite	B although	C besides	D unless
5	A claimed	B told	C pretended	D related
6	A allow	B permit	C let	D enable
7	A interested	B fond	C enthusiastic	D keen
8	A make	B allow	C let	D learn
9	A change	B make	C let	D turn
10	A take	B put	C set	D bring
11	A Although	B In spite	C Even though	D Despite
12	A shy	B timid	C withdrawn	D outgoing
13	A conceited	B arrogant	C proud	D shy
14	A long	B high	C tall	D great
15	A surprising	B surprised	C interested	D interesting

UNIT 10

A Reading

Read the article about the relationship between humans and animals. Five sentences have been removed from the article. Choose from sentences A–F the one which fits each gap (1–4). There is one extra sentence which you do not need. There is an example at the beginning (0).

MAKING SENSE OF MONKEY BUSINESS

'Who can one hit, if not one's friends?' a famous actor once asked his old comrade and fellow actor shortly before punching him on the jaw.

The response of the surprised, bruised actor is not recorded. Nevertheless, the story illustrates an interesting aspect of human behaviour. **0** *D* Peace was made – and this reconciliation represents the most important aspect of the incident, says Dutch zoologist Frans de Waal in a recently-published book.

He believes that scientists who study human nature have concentrated on violence, on our ability for competition, at the expense of our capacity for making peace. **1** ____ An examination of reconciliation is needed to correct the balance, he believes.

De Waal has studied human peacemaking and has attempted to put it in its proper context – by comparing how we and our close animal cousins, the apes and monkeys, solve our disputes.

2 ____ It is, however, a dangerous approach, for it is all too easy to detect human 'motivation' in creatures incapable of such experiences.

But for de Waal, such comparisons are not invalid. The only differences in behaviour, he believes, are those of time. **3** ____ Our species has many conciliatory gestures in common with these animals, e.g. stretching out a hand, smiling, kissing, embracing – which de Waal traces back 30 million years. So what does this new interpretation of human reconciliation tell us about world conflicts, peace negotiations and arms reduction talks? Unfortunately, not much, it seems.

'If my studies of monkeys and apes contain any lesson for the world, it is that people who need each other for one reason or another are less likely to fight: and, if they do fight, they are more likely to make up afterwards.' **4** ____ Nevertheless, it would be wrong to criticize such an interesting book for this reason.

A Dutch zoologist Frans de Waal was reluctant to explain his theories.

B The result is a highly readable book which emphasizes the parallels between our behaviour and that of animals.

C As a result, these scientists have led people to believe that violence is much more a part of human nature than peace.

D Despite the unreasonable attack, the two old men remained firm friends.

E It is a message unlikely to revolutionize world politics.

F Whereas monkeys generally make up within minutes, humans can take years to do the same.

B Vocabulary 1

Can you write in the opposites of these words? There may be more than one possible answer. The first one has been done for you.

happy	*sad, unhappy*
bored	____
tolerant	____
even-tempered	____
patient	____
brave/courageous	____
sensitive	____
unashamed	____
sincere	____
observant	____
important	____
legible	____
obedient	____

C Vocabulary 2

Arrange the different kinds of feelings below under the appropriate headings in the table. Then use one of the words in its correct form in sentences 1–10.

contentment	delight	contempt	boredom
shock	pleasure	disgust	happiness
anger	astonishment	joy	amazement
surprise	approval	fear	amusement
sadness			

Unfavourable	Unfavourable or favourable	Favourable

1 To my ________, he arrived unexpectedly on the doorstep with a huge bunch of flowers.

2 Children of all ages can enjoy themselves in ________ parks.

3 During the school holidays he suffered from intense ________ as all his friends were away.

4 Her parents happily gave their ________ when she told them she wanted to marry Jim.

5 He raised his fist in ________ at the driver who had just crashed into him.

6 The death of a loved one causes great ________ .

7 Many people suffer from a ________ of heights.

8 It gives me great ________ to present you with this prize for achievement.

9 For many people a simple life is the best way to find true ________ .

10 He was a very superior man, who always treated other people with ________ .

D Language study 1

Fill in the missing words in the table. Then complete the sentences below with an appropriate form of the word in brackets.

Adjective	Comparative	Superlative
________	better	________
easy	________	________
much/many	________	________
________	________	most interesting
________	________	fastest
bad	________	________
________	larger	________
thin	________	________
________	harder	________
unusual	________	________
pretty	________	________
________	more expensive	________

1 Learning to speak a language is often much ________(easy) than learning to write it.

2 This hotel must be ________(expensive) than the small one next door.

3 An orange is ________(large) than a plum.

4 He is certainly the ________(unusual) person I have ever met.

5 Bringing up children is one of the ________(hard) jobs in the world.

6 His latest film was ________(interesting) than his previous ones.

7 What is the ________(difficult) thing you have ever done?

8 When I saw her, she looked much ________(thin) than I remembered her.

9 Losing your credit card is ________(bad) than losing your money.

10 This is the ________(fast) car we produce.

E Phrasal verbs

Rewrite these sentences using the word in bold. There is an example at the beginning (0).

(0) 'The RSPCA is the Royal Society for the Prevention of Cruelty to Animals.'

stand

The letters RSPCA *stand for* the Royal Society for the Prevention of Cruelty to Animals.

1 I don't think John will ever recover from the shock of his wife's death.

get

John will ________________ the shock of his wife's death.

2 I'm sorry to say that the job really depresses me.

gets

The job ________________, I'm afraid.

3 Peter has very little money but he manages to make ends meet.

gets

Peter ________________ very little money.

4 It's a pity but the boss and her personal assistant really detest each other.

well

The boss and her personal assistant ________________ at all, I'm afraid.

5 Some young people like to wear clothes that will be noticed in a crowd.

stand

Some young people like to dress so that they ________________ in a crowd.

6 It is often difficult to face bullies at school.

stand

School children often find it difficult to ________________ bullies.

7 Thieves forced their way into the bank last night.

broke

Thieves ________________ the bank last night.

8 Recovering from a serious illness can take a long time.

get

It can take a long time ________________ a serious illness.

F Language study 2

Make sentences using the prompts to show what you generally prefer and what you would rather have on a specific occasion.

Example:
tea/coffee/tea late at night
I prefer (drinking) tea to (drinking) coffee but I'd rather have / drink tea late at night.

> ***Remember:*** we use *prefer* for more general statements and *would rather* for more specific choices.

1 TV/the cinema/go to the cinema tonight

____

2 flying/driving/drive to Manchester tomorrow

____

3 the country/the town/spend this weekend in town

____

4 a cold climate/a hot climate/have a holiday in the sun this year

____

5 meat/fish/have the fish in this restaurant

____

6 smart clothes/casual clothes/wear jeans at the weekend

____

7 large cars/small cars/a small car in the city

____

8 long hair/short hair/have shorter hair in the summer

____

G Use of English

Read the letter below and think of one word which best fits each space. There is an example at the beginning (0).

Dear John,

How are you? Thanks very (0) *much* for your letter and all your news. I apologise (1)________ not replying sooner, but I've (2)________ busy looking for a new job. The old one was really getting me down, I'm afraid, and I was ready for (3)________ change. I just didn't get (4)________ well with my old boss – we didn't see eye to eye on anything! In desperation I got in touch (5)________ this employment bureau, WPA (that stands for 'Work Placement Agency', (6)________ the way!). Well, (7)________ my surprise, they contacted me almost immediately and asked if I (8)________ like to go for an interview for a job that I was really interested in. I've just heard this morning (9)________ I got the job! To celebrate, I'm inviting a (10)________ friends to a small party next Saturday night. Do come, and, (11)________ you like, bring your new girl-friend. I'd like to meet her. I'm not sure how (12)________ people will be coming yet, but it should be fun! Let me know whether you can make it or not, just (13)________ case I end up inviting too many people! The flat's not big (14)________ for a huge crowd! Looking forward to seeing you. It seems ages (15)________ we saw each other last!

Yours,

Sally

H Language study 3

Match comments 1–6 with the speaker's intentions a–f.

1 I'm very grateful for all your help.
2 I'm afraid we'll be busy on the 3rd.
3 We were so sorry to hear your sad news.
4 I can't say how sorry I am. I didn't mean to offend you.
5 We'd like you to come too, if you can make it.
6 We were delighted to hear about your engagement.
7 If you like, I can bring a picnic.

a Expressing sympathy
b Making an invitation
c Expressing thanks
d Apologising
e Congratulating
f Refusing an invitation
g Making a suggestion

PROGRESS TEST 2

A Vocabulary cloze

Decide which word, A, B, C or D, best fits each space. There is an example at the beginning (0).

Hooked on the Net

The (0) *latest* addiction to trap thousands of people is the Internet, which has been (1)_____ for broken relationships, job losses, financial ruin and even one suicide. Psychologists now recognize Internet Addiction Syndrome (IAS) as a new illness that could (2)_____ serious problems and ruin many lives. Special help groups have been set up to (3)_____ sufferers help and support.

Psychologists have described many (4)_____ examples, including one man who took his own life after (5)_____ more than £14,000 to feed his addiction, and a teenager who had to receive psychiatric treatment for his 12-hour-a-day (6)_____ . 'This illness is not (7)_____ , and it must be taken seriously,' said an expert in behavioural addiction at Nottingham Trent University. 'These are not sad people with serious personality (8)_____ ; they are people who were fine before they found the Internet.'

IAS is similar to other problems like gambling, smoking and drinking: addicts have dreams about the Internet; they need to use it first thing in the morning; they (9)_____ to their partners about how much time they spend online; they (10)_____ they could cut down, but are unable to do so. A recent study found that many users spend up to 40 hours a week on the Internet; (11)_____ they felt guilty, they became depressed if they were (12)_____ to stop using it.

Almost anyone can be at risk. Some of the addicts are teenagers who are already (13)_____ on computer games and who (14)_____ it very difficult to resist the games on the Internet. Surprisingly, however, psychologists (15)_____ that most victims are middle-aged housewives who have never used a computer before.

0	A closest	B latest	C nearest	D soonest
1	A blamed	B faulted	C mistaken	D accused
2	A lead	B affect	C take	D cause
3	A offer	B suggest	C recommend	D advise
4	A worrying	B worried	C disappointing	D disappointed
5	A gaining	B lending	C winning	D borrowing
6	A habit	B custom	C manner	D routine
7	A false	B imitation	C fake	D artificial
8	A mistakes	B errors	C faults	D defects
9	A betray	B deceive	C cheat	D lie
10	A want	B wish	C rather	D prefer
11	A although	B despite	C unless	D without
12	A let	B allowed	C had	D made
13	A taken	B addicted	C tied	D hooked
14	A say	B feel	C find	D have
15	A promise	B tell	C say	D object

B Open cloze

Think of ONE word which best fits each space. There is an example at the beginning (0).

Taking it easy

Society has changed (0) *in* many ways (1)_______ the introduction of computers, and people's lives at home and at the office have been affected. Most people are working for fewer hours per week than they (2)_______ to, and manufacturers and advertising agencies are becoming much (3)_______ interested in how people spend this extra leisure time. One recent report stated that, (4)_______ the number of hobbies had not increased, each hobby (5)_______ become much more specialized.

A second finding is that nowadays, many managers would (6)_______ spend time with their families (7)_______ stay late in the office every day. Home life is seen to be just as important (8)________ working. Some companies now (9)________ managers take their annual holidays even if they don't want to, because this leads to (10)________ an improvement in their performance if they have some rest.

In (11)________ of these changes, some people are working harder than ever before. The standard of exams is getting higher, and increased competition is (12)________ it harder to get into university than it was 20 years (13)________. Schoolchildren and students are now having to work (14)________ hard that in many cases they work longer hours (15)________ their parents.

C Key word transformations

Rewrite the sentences using the word in bold.

1 I haven't seen Nella for two years.

last

It's two ________________ Nella.

2 Michelle sings so well that she is never short of work.

such

Michelle ________________ that she is never short of work.

3 Although her leg hurt, Amanda finished the race.

pain

In ________________ her leg, Amanda finished the race.

4 It is such a pity that I can't go to the party.

could

I ________________ to the party.

5 I wasn't interested in the film so I turned the TV off.

find

I didn't ________________, so I turned the TV off.

6 I regret ever meeting you.

wish

I ________________ you.

7 Your results never improve because you don't work hard.

if

Your results ________________ harder.

8 She says I caused the accident.

blames

She ________________ the accident.

9 John said he was sorry that he had arrived late.

apologised

John ________________ late.

10 Haven't you found a house yet?

still

Are ________________ a house?

D Error correction

In the following text, some lines contain a mistake. Tick the lines that are correct and underline the words that you do not need. There are two examples at the beginning (0) and (00).

Keeping your distance

0 *Personal space* is a term that refers to the distance we ✓
00 like <u>for</u> to keep between ourselves and other people.
1 When someone we do not know well gets too close that
2 we usually begin to feel uncomfortable. If such a
3 business colleague comes more closer than 1.2 metres,
4 the most common response is to move away.
5 Some interesting studies have been done in libraries. If
6 strangers will come too close, many people get up and
7 leave the building; others use to different methods
8 such as turning their back on the intruder.
9 Living in cities has made people to develop new skills for
10 dealing with situations where they are very close to
11 strangers. Most people on so crowded trains try not to
12 look at strangers; they avoid skin contact, and are
13 apologise if hands touch by a mistake. People use
14 newspapers as a barrier between themselves and other
15 people, and if they still do not have one, they stare into
the distance, making sure they are not looking into
anyone's eyes.

UNIT 11

A Reading

Read the text and choose the best answer in 1–6.

You tell us your real-life experiences

what it's like ...

Whirlwind Romances

It's the stuff Mills and Boon novels are made of – being taken off into the sunset by the man of your dreams who you only met half an hour ago! But surely whirlwind romances never happen in real life? Jeanette Baker spoke to a reader who can safely say that they do!

FIONA, 22, from Kirby, had had proposals of marriage in the past but it wasn't until she met her friend's boyfriend that she knew the right person had come along.

'Tim was going out with a friend of mine when I was introduced to him last November. There was an instant attraction, and although I know it was unfair to my friend, that January we started to have a relationship.

Tim's girlfriend soon realized that something was going wrong with her relationship with Tim and that they were drifting apart. As he was going to Moscow for a fortnight in February, she asked him if he was seeing someone else. He confirmed that it was over between them, and they split up. Once he was free from that commitment, we started going out and spent every day together in the week before he went away.

I couldn't believe how much I missed him when he was in Moscow even though I'd only known him for six weeks or how deeply I had fallen in love with him. I even said to friends while he was away, 'This is the man I am going to marry.' I was slightly nervous when he came back because I wasn't sure if he felt the same way or if he had even missed me. I needn't have worried – the weekend after he came back, he proposed. He said he couldn't bear to be away from me again and wanted to be with me for the rest of his life. I know it may sound old-fashioned, but that's exactly how we both felt. We got engaged and decided to have the ceremony as quickly as possible.

The date was set for the end of March – three weeks away, and it was supposed to be a very small affair – just me and him. We knew it was a terrible rush – but that's how we wanted it. Everyone was amazed. By the time I introduced Tim to my parents it was only two weeks to the wedding, so I suppose they knew they had no say in the matter and that we were serious.

When we got married, what was supposed to be a small affair turned out to be about 50 people packed into the Registry Office. I definitely think that when you meet the right person you know immediately that he's right, and Tim was the first man I could ever imagine myself growing old with.

People had proposed to me before, but, though I'd accepted, doubts came into my mind afterwards or it just didn't work out. With Tim I can safely say that I've never considered for a moment not spending the rest of my life with him.'

1 When Fiona started going out with Tim,
- A she had just broken up with a boyfriend.
- B he was still going out with another girl.
- C he had just come back from abroad.
- D she was going out with a friend of his.

2 When Tim was away, Fiona
- A told her friend he had asked her to marry him.
- B missed him more than she had expected.
- C spent a long time deciding whether to marry him.
- D did not think about him very much.

3 Fiona felt nervous about seeing Tim again because
- A she thought he had met someone new.
- B she wanted to ask him to marry her.
- C she was afraid he might ask her to marry him.
- D she did not know if he shared her feelings.

4 When Tim met Fiona's parents for the first time
- A it was two weeks after the wedding.
- B it was too late for them to object to the wedding.
- C they warned him not to rush into getting married.
- D they did not believe that Tim and Fiona were serious.

5 It would appear from the text that Fiona
- A had doubts about marrying Tim.
- B had previously agreed to marry someone else.
- C was not allowed to get married in a church.
- D was not immediately sure whether Tim was right for her.

6 Fiona and Tim were probably chosen as the subject of the article because
- A they got married when they were young.
- B they were separated shortly after they had met.
- C they got married so soon after meeting each other.
- D they had to hurt a friend to get what they wanted.

B Vocabulary

Look at the list of expressions showing different stages of a relationship. Try to put them in the order they might happen by writing the numbers 1–13 beside them. Then use the expressions to fill in the spaces in the text below.

to drift apart from someone	to get married to someone
to live apart from someone	to go out with someone
to be introduced to someone	to get divorced from someone
to split up with someone	to propose to someone
to be attracted to someone	to have a date with someone
to fall in love with someone	to get engaged to someone
to chat someone up	

Helen and John's story, although sad, is not an unusual one. It began well enough, when they were both eighteen. They (1)__________ to each other at a party given by a mutual friend. Helen was looking her best, and it was fairly clear to everyone that John (2)__________ her because he spent the whole evening (3)__________ her up and hardly talked to anyone else all evening. They arranged to (4)__________ , and within a few weeks, they were (5)__________ each other seriously.

Although it wasn't love at first sight, it didn't take long for them to (6)__________ . One romantic summer evening, when they were walking by the river in the moonlight, John (7)__________ to her and she accepted. The next day they arranged a party to tell everyone that they had (8)__________.

They (9)__________ in church a few months later, and for the first year, everything went well. But in time, they both changed and became interested in different things. They slowly (10)__________ apart, and one day they realized that they were not suited to each other. They agreed that the best thing would be for them to (11)__________ up. So John moved out, and after they had started (12)__________ apart, they realized that it had been a mistake to get married so young. In the end they (13)__________ , and now they both live alone.

C Language Study 1

Change these questions into indirect questions using the word in bold.

1 In your opinion, should they get married?
think
Do ______________ get married?

2 What time is the wedding taking place? Do you know?
when
Do you ______________ taking place?

3 Did they get married in church? Do you know?
if
Do you ______________ in church?

4 Where will they go for their honeymoon? What do you think?
think
Where ______________ go for their honeymoon?

5 When is their anniversary exactly? Do you know?
when
Do you know ______________ exactly?

6 What did Laura wear at the wedding? Can you remember?
what
Can you ______________ at the wedding?

7 In your opinion, are they suited to each other?
think
Do you ______________ to each other?

8 Why did Helen break up with John? Do you know?
why
Do you know ______________ John?

D Use of English 1

Read the text about a wedding and decide which word, A, B, C or D, best fits each space. There is an example at the beginning (0).

Janet got (0)*married* to Pedro last Saturday, and we went to the (1)______ , which (2)______ place in a lovely little church in the country. Janet, the (3)______ , wore a beautiful white dress; it had a long train made of silk, and it was carried by a young (4)______ , who was the daughter of her elder sister. At the start, her husband-to-be, the (5)______ , was waiting for her at the front of the church. She walked down the aisle to the front with her father, and after the (6)______ , she came back down again with her husband.

Afterwards, people (7)______ photos outside the church, and all the (8)______ were invited to a (9)______ in a hotel nearby, where we all had a meal. During the meal, the (10)______ man, who was Pedro's oldest friend, made a lovely (11)______ , and told everyone about how they had met, what it was like when they first started (12)______ out, and what Pedro had said when he had (13)______ . Then a few hours later, they set off on their (14)______ , which they were going to (15)______ in Bali.

0	A wedded	B engaged	C married	D proposed
1	A engagement	B proposal	C marriage	D wedding
2	A found	B held	C took	D stood
3	A lady	B groom	C maid	D bride
4	A bridesmaid	B bridegroom	C bride	D groom
5	A male	B man	C groom	D bride
6	A ceremony	B party	C celebration	D custom
7	A made	B did	C shot	D took
8	A guests	B members	C spectators	D viewers
9	A reception	B meeting	C greeting	D date
10	A first	B best	C top	D greatest
11	A talk	B lecture	C story	D speech
12	A leaving	B setting	C going	D dating
13	A proposed	B engaged	C suggested	D intended
14	A holiday	B honeymoon	C festival	D carnival
15	A take	B spend	C pass	D get

E Language study 2

Read the letter. Put the verbs in either the *-ing* form or the infinitive. The first one has been done for you.

My darling,

I miss (0)___*being*___(be) with you so much. I know I ought to enjoy (1)__________(travel) through Europe with my parents, but I just can't help (2)__________(think) about you all the time. I know they want me (3)__________(be) happy, but I just feel like (4)__________(come) home to you. I've considered (5)__________(tell) them what the matter is, but I don't want (6)__________(risk) (7)__________(make) them angry, because they are trying so hard (8)__________(make) me happy.

Tomorrow we have decided (9)__________(go) to Rome and then we're planning (10)__________(visit) Venice for a few days. After that we've arranged (11)__________(stay) in France for a couple of weeks, but I hope (12)__________(get) back before the end of the month.

I promise (13)__________(write) to you every day. I'm looking forward (14)__________(see) you again so much that you wouldn't believe it.

I miss you.

Love, J

F Language study 3

Fill in the spaces in these sentences with the verb in either the *-ing* form or infinitive.

1 I don't know how the accident happened. I remember __________(feel) very tired, but that's all. The rest is a complete blank.

2 Oh good. I'm glad you remembered __________(get) Helen a card. We can post it this evening.

3 Although I don't look forward to it, I like __________(go) to the dentist every three months for a check-up in case I need any fillings.

4 I like __________(cook), but I also enjoy meals out at restaurants.

5 I'll never forget __________(meet) the Queen. It was a wonderful experience.

6 He had to go back to the supermarket because he had forgotten __________(get) any butter.

7 On his way home, he stopped at the newsagent __________(buy) a paper.

8 I wish it would stop __________(rain).

9 I regret __________(say) that I won't be able to come to the party, but I hope you have a great time.

10 After three months without work, he regretted __________(leave) his safe job at the bank.

G Use of English 2

Rewrite these sentences using the word in bold.

1 I don't find it hard to get up early.
used
I ______________ up early.

2 The police officers forced him to sign the confession.
made
The police officers ______________ the confession.

3 What did John think of the film? Do you know?
what
Do you ______________ of the film?

4 I'd be happy to give you a lift.
mind
I ______________ a lift.

5 Smoking at our school is not allowed.
let
They ______________ at school.

6 He had no idea she would be so pretty.
than
She was much ______________ she would be.

7 He found the exam surprisingly easy.
much
The exam was ______________ expected.

8 I was very surprised when they got married.
thought
I never ______________ married.

9 I lived in London once, but I don't any more.
used
I ______________ in London.

10 I no longer speak to my neighbour since our quarrel.
stopped
I ______________ to my neighbour since our quarrel.

H Use of English 3

Read the text. If a line is correct, put a tick (✓). If a line has an unnecessary word, underline it. There are two examples at the beginning (0) and (00).

0 As he sat in his room, Mark looked at the photograph ✓
00 of Sally, and his eyes began to fill of with tears. He
1 remembered meeting her for the first time outside of
2 the library, and thought of their walks through the park
3 and their first kiss. It had been love at the first sight
4 for both of them; neither of them had ever expected
5 that it would be end, but somehow it had all gone
6 to wrong and she had left.
7 Now, three years later, he still bitterly regretted letting
8 her to go. At first he had thought he would soon get
9 used to living without her. But weeks passed, then
10 months and years and if anything else, the pain got
11 worse rather than more better.
12 He decided himself to go for a walk and went towards the
13 bridge by the river where he had proposed to her there.
14 Then suddenly, as he turned the corner round, he
15 froze, and for a moment short, he could not breathe.
There was a woman sitting alone on the riverbank by the
bridge. It was her.

UNIT 12

A Reading 1

Read the text and choose the best answer in 1–7.

'Oh, you're so lucky living in Bath, it's such a wonderful, lovely, historic place,' people say enthusiastically, and all you can think of is the awful parking, the crowds of tourists, the expensive shops, the narrow-minded council, and the terrible traffic ...

Luckily I don't live in Bath but nearly ten miles away in a village called Limpley Stoke in the Avon Valley. It seems to be normal in the countryside these days for professional people who work in the town to prefer to live in the villages; this makes the housing so expensive that the villagers and agricultural workers have to live in the cheaper accommodation in town, with the result that the farmers commute out to the farm and everyone else commutes in. Certainly, there's nobody in the village who could be called an old-style villager. The people nearest to me include a pilot, an accountant, a British Rail manager, a retired teacher ... not a farm worker amongst them. But I don't think there is anything wrong with that – it's just that the nature of villages is changing and there is still quite a strong sense of community here. A lot of this sense of community comes from the Post Office, which is a centre for all the gossip and information. I find out what is going on while I am there, pretending to control my two-year-old son. He enjoys anything he can touch at the lowest level of the shop, which consists mainly of an enormous rack of cards saying 'Congratulations on your 9th Birthday' and a collecting tin for the 'Save The Children' charity, which he always picks up and tries to run away with. My feeling is that if my son took the money collected for the children, it would go directly where it was needed but they don't see it like that.

Working at home, I tend to wander round the village at times when other people are at the office, which has given me a reputation for being incredibly lazy or unbelievably rich, but I still don't get enough time to look after the garden we bought. My wife had a good idea for the first year. 'Let's just leave it and see what comes up.' There were some nice plants among the weeds. She had a good idea for the second year as well. 'Why don't we leave it and see if it all comes up again?' We did, and that is why we need to hire a full-time gardener this year.

1 What is the author's attitude to Bath?
  A It is a wonderful place to live in.
  B It has far too many disadvantages.
  C He feels fortunate to live there.
  D It has many good shops.

2 The people who live in the village
  A tend to work on the farms.
  B are mostly professionals who work in the town.
  C are unable to afford houses in the town.
  D don't like the old-style villagers.

3 It would appear from the text that the Post Office
  A sells a wide range of cards.
  B is where most of the charity work is organized.
  C is a place where villagers can talk to each other.
  D sells a range of tinned food as well as stamps.

4 The author has a reputation for being lazy as he
  A only works during the mornings.
  B spends a lot of time shopping with his son.
  C likes to walk around the village.
  D seems to be free when people are working.

5 The garden is not in very good condition because
  A the author is too lazy to look after it.
  B the author cannot afford to pay a gardener.
  C the author's wife has no interest in it.
  D nobody has worked on it for over two years.

6 The author feels that living in the village
  A is better than living in Bath.
  B has a number of disadvantages.
  C tends to be rather dull.
  D is something that everyone would enjoy.

B Vocabulary 1

Below are six words from the text, but the letters are in the wrong order. Find the hidden words and match them with the definitions 1–10.

teedirr	somenour	utcemom
aendwr	lfwau	pigsos

1	______________	terrible
2	______________	to travel to town to go to work every day
3	______________	having stopped work at the age of 60 or 65
4	______________	news and talk about what people are doing
5	______________	very big
6	______________	to walk around with no particular destination

C Language study 1

Take one idea from the left column and one from the right column to complete the sentences using *not only …* .

Example:
looked different — voice had changed

I didn't recognize him at all; … *not only did he look different, but his voice had changed as well.*

beaches are wonderful broke his leg food was awful speak the language speaks fluent French train was crowded	have lived in Moscow weather is lovely speaks perfect German train arrived late sprained his wrist waiters were very rude

1 I would definitely recommend Greece for a holiday; ______________________

2 He had the most terrible journey home; ______________________

3 I consider myself to be an expert on Russia; ______________________

4 She's completely bilingual; ______________________

5 He had a bad skiing accident last year; ______________________

6 I will never go to that restaurant again; ______________________

D Language study 2

Rewrite these sentences with the correct form of *have something done.* Use the word in bold.

Example:
Where can I take my shoes for mending round here?
have
Where can I *have my shoes mended round here*?

1 Where did he take his car for a service last week?
have
Where did ______________ last week?

2 My sister went to the optician's for an eye test.
tested
My sister ______________ at the optician's.

3 Can I bring my film for developing here?
have
Can ______________ here?

4 Candy's getting them to decorate the house soon.
have
Candy's going ______________ soon.

5 Sue gets someone in Paris to make her clothes.
made
Sue ______________ in Paris.

6 Which hairdresser's did Helen go to last week?
cut
Where did Helen ______________ last week?

E Vocabulary 2

Complete the sentences with the correct form of *make* or *do.*

1 I'd like to _____ an appointment to see the doctor.

2 Why haven't you _____ the washing up yet?

3 If you aren't _____ anything this weekend, would you like to come round for dinner?

4 What did he _____ at university? Was it Law?

5 My father is too busy _____ money to enjoy himself.

6 Don't _____ any noise or you'll wake the children.

7 She had to type the letter again because she had _____ so many mistakes.

8 Harry's mother knew what to do when he broke his arm because she _____ a course in First Aid.

9 She's happier now that she has _____ a few friends.

10 You're very lucky that you don't have to _____ military service in England.

F Use of English

Read the text and think of ONE word which best fits each space. There is an example at the beginning (0).

Amelia Earhart, America's most famous woman pilot, was born into a wealthy family (0)__*in*__ 1897. At the age of 23, she began taking flying lessons in California. In (1)________ of having a number of crashes, (2)________ were fairly common in the early days of aviation, she decided (3)________ make flying her career.

In 1932 she became the first woman to make a solo flight across the Atlantic. She set out on May 20th, and (4)________ only did she succeed in arriving safely, (5)________ she managed to do it in record time as (6)________ . She (7)________ awarded honours of all kinds. As her fame grew, she travelled round the country giving lectures and promoting women's rights.

In 1937, she decided to (8)________ something that no woman had tried before – to fly all the way round the world. She reached Australia, and set (9)________ on the last part of her journey across the Pacific (10)________ July 2nd. A few hours later, she sent a radio message saying she was running short (11)________ fuel. Then there was silence. President Roosevelt immediately (12)________ the area searched, but the 9 ships and 66 planes were unable to find any sign of her.

Since her death, (13)________ have been many stories about her; some say that she was captured by the Japanese, others claim that she lived on a South Pacific island with a fisherman. However, (14)________ many people have tried to work out exactly what happened, (15)________ trace of her or the plane has ever been found.

G Reading 2

Read the text on the right about places to stay on Lundy Island. Then answer questions 1–14, writing A–F beside each question. There is an example at the beginning (0).

Which section mentions:

how to get to the island?	0	*B*
a house that would be suitable for a single person?	1	
a house that has been divided into two?	2	
where the island is?	3	
a relatively new house?	4	
how much it costs to stay there?	5	
a house with a unique view?	6	
the number of people who live on Lundy?	7	
what you can do when you are there?	8	
a house that is particularly warm?	9	
where people are allowed to walk?	10	
a house that is on its own?	11	
how big the island is?	12	
a house that is protected from the wind?	13	
the amount of traffic there is?	14	

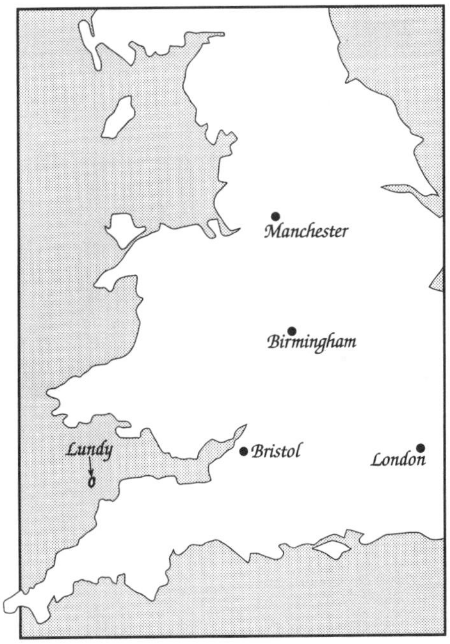

A Lundy Island The island of Lundy, set in the Atlantic Ocean about fifteen miles off the west coast of Devon, is three miles long and rises over four hundred feet out of the sea. It has tremendous views towards England, Wales and across the Atlantic. It has tall cliffs towards the south and west, and small wooded valleys on the east coast facing the mainland. There are three lighthouses, a castle, a church, a farm, several houses and cottages, a population of about fifteen, and no cars. Most of the buildings are made of the island's beautiful light-coloured stone.

B Staying on Lundy Lundy offers visitors a rare experience. It is large enough to have a life of its own which visitors can share, but small enough to be like a different world. Visitors are free to go anywhere, and can wander alone along the clifftops in silence or spend time with other people in the pub and shop.
Our ship, the MS Oldenburg, runs throughout the year. On the island we have made it possible for people to stay at varying levels of price and comfort – in houses, hostels, small cottages or camping – so that almost anyone can afford to be here.

The Properties

C The Old Light The lighthouse, the keeper's house and the store were designed by Daniel Alexander and built in 1820. The lighthouse stands on the highest point of the island. The keeper's house is divided into two flats for four and five people. The upper flat (with five beds) is the only building in Lundy that has views to the north of the island.

D Old Light Cottage This used to be the lighthouse keeper's store, and is solidly built of stone. We have equipped it with a bed, small kitchen and bathroom for those who come to Lundy on their own. It stands near the lighthouse, and has in it just about everything that one person could want.

E Square Cottage was completely re-built by us on the remains of a 19th century house. It has wonderful views, especially from the upstairs sitting room, which has a lovely Victorian fireplace. It also has central heating, using up surplus energy from the island's generator, and so is very comfortable in winter.

F Hanmers was built by a fisherman in 1902. He chose a good site, a dip in the hill, on the path from the beach to the castle, so the place is isolated and sheltered, but has the usual wonderful views towards the sea. The interior is of wood, painted white in the front rooms, which gives it a cosy and solid feel.

UNIT 13

A Reading

Read the article on self-help advice for those at risk of spending too much. For questions 1–7, choose from the sections of the article (A–F). Some of the sections may be chosen more than once. There is an example at the beginning (0).

Self-help advice

A Ask yourself what is missing in your life. What kind of emotional gap are you trying to fill? Does shopping distract you from problems you would prefer not to have to think about? Recognizing the reasons for your problem is the first step towards solving it.

B If it is your partner's earnings you spend, rather than your own, are you feeling angry or resentful towards your partner for some reason? If so, ask yourself why, and try to do something constructive about it – perhaps discussing the problem with your partner or a friend.

C If you buy gifts compulsively, you need to learn to express your love in other ways. You should also think about why you feel the need to 'buy' other people's love.

D If you buy compulsively for yourself, it may be a sign of feeling emotionally deprived. Try to find other ways of 'giving' to yourself which are less self-destructive such as a walk in the park, a hot bath, or talking to a friend. Also, try to ensure your emotional needs are met, with help from your partner or through friends.

E If you cannot trust yourself at the moment, destroy tempting credit cards, and leave your cheque book at home until you've sorted out your underlying emotional problems.

F If your spending frightens you and you are worried it may be out of control, ask your doctor to refer you to a clinical psychologist for a course of specialist help.

Which paragraph advises you to:

seek medical help if you can't stop spending?	0	*F*
try to satisfy your emotional needs in ways that do not involve buying yourself presents?	1	
decide whether you are spending someone else's money simply to hurt that person?	2	
find out what is wrong in your life?	3	
get rid of anything that encourages you to buy on credit?	4	
talk to someone about your problem?	5	
try doing different things to show your feelings to people you love?	6	
look for an explanation for your compulsive habit?	7	

B Vocabulary 1

Some prepositions are missing in these sentences. Can you fill the spaces?

1. These goods were previously on sale ________ a higher price.
2. Samples will be provided ________ request.
3. Refunds will be made ________ proof of purchase.
4. Customers are requested to refrain ________ smoking in this area.
5. Refunds ________ excess of £20 cannot be made without a receipt.
6. Refunds will not be given ________ respect of soiled or damaged goods.
7. Customers are requested to leave their bags at the desk when trying ________ footwear.
8. The management accepts no responsibility ________ accidents.
9. This garment will fade ________ repeated washing.
10. If you find an item purchased here on sale anywhere else at lower price, we will make ________ the difference.

C Use of English 1

Read the text and decide which word, A, B, C or D, best fits each space. There is an example at the beginning (0).

Have you (0) *ever* noticed how compulsive shoppers are never in a (1)_____ when they are hunting for something to buy? Now, I don't want to be (2)_____ to these people, but it has always struck me that this sort of person must, in (3)_____ ways, be able to put up (4)_____ the most incredible boredom. I, myself, am an extremely reluctant shopper. I only have to (5)_____ a glimpse of the window of a large department (6)_____ as I flash past in a taxi and I am immediately seized by a desire to be a million miles away.

To be (7)_____, I think it has something to (8)_____ with the fact that I was once wrongly (9)_____ of shop-lifting. It goes without saying that I was completely innocent of the charge of (10)_____ anything, but the experience (11)_____ me with the feeling that I wanted to (12)_____ the manager for wrongful arrest. I (13)_____ to think what might have happened (14)_____ I had actually been wrongly convicted. Even now I sometimes have nightmares about (15)_____ in vain to ruthless detectives that I was not a shop-lifter.

0 A yet	B ever	C still	D always
1 A dash	B run	C race	D hurry
2 A violent	B severe	C stern	D unkind
3 A any	B the	C few	D some
4 A for	B with	C in	D by
5 A see	B catch	C notice	D look
6 A store	B shop	C market	D stall
7 A true	B decent	C reliable	D honest
8 A be	B do	C put	D go
9 A charged	B accused	C blamed	D criticized
10 A robbery	B theft	C stealing	D robbing
11 A gave	B left	C made	D caused
12 A claim	B sue	C try	D compensate
13 A fear	B worry	C dread	D resist
14 A whether	B unless	C when	D if
15 A expressing	B opposing	C protesting	D arguing

D Use of English 2

Read the text and think of one word which best fits each space. There is an example at the beginning (0).

'Don't miss this discount...'

Harold and Betty Prior asked the representative of a fitted kitchen company to call (0) *at* the flat they had bought for their retirement. The woman arrived at 6.30 p.m., before the Priors had eaten, and left (1)_______ before midnight. 'By the end of that time we felt completely worn out,' recalls Betty. The woman spent some time talking (2)_______ the company and how it (3)_______ grown over the years. She then went into the kitchen to measure up. This (4)_______ just 15 minutes. When she came out, she drew up plans and announced (5)_______ the units would cost £9,000.

'She told us the special offer that month was a dishwasher, but she (6)_______ see we already had one. Then she said (7)_______ we signed before Saturday – in two days' (8)_______, we could have £2,000 off. I was rather surprised by this, as (9)_______ dishwasher is worth £2,000.

'I told her it (10)_______ impossible for us to make up our minds that quickly. So she said that if we signed a piece of paper and paid a deposit of £100 the offer (11)_______ remain open for another week.'

The Priors were determined to shop around first and (12)_______ woman finally left without an order. But they believe (13)_______ less strong-minded people might well have given in to her technique: 'We (14)_______ exhausted by that stage. I'm sure some people would (15)_______ been worn down,' says Betty.

E Language study 1

Complete sentences 1–8 using a relative pronoun where necessary.

Examples:

They asked round a kitchen company representative. She arrived at 6.30.
The kitchen company representative they asked round arrived at 6.30.

The woman arrived at 6.30. She left just before midnight.
The woman, who arrived at 6.30, left just before midnight.

> ***Remember:*** you can leave out the relative pronoun only when it refers to the *object* of the verb in the clause.

1 The woman spent fifteen minutes measuring the kitchen. She talked to the Priors.
The woman ______________________________

____

2 The woman drew up some plans. They were for a new kitchen.
The plans ______________________________

____

3 The Priors were interested in some units. They would cost £9,000.
The units ______________________________

____

4 A dishwasher was on special offer that month. It was not needed by the Priors.
The dishwasher ______________________________

____

5 The Priors signed a piece of paper. It entitled them to a discount of £2,000.
The piece ______________________________

____

6 The woman asked for a deposit. It was for £100.
The deposit ______________________________

____

7 The woman worked for a man. He would have been furious if she had not obtained the order.
The man ______________________________

____

8 Some people are not so strong-minded. They would probably place an order.
People ______________________________

____

F Vocabulary 2

Choose the correct prefix from the following list to make the opposite of the words below.

non-	un-	in-	il-
mis-	im-	dis-	ir-

pack	__________	expected	__________
agree	__________	spell	__________
proper	__________	possible	__________
likely	__________	dependent	__________
sense	__________	usual	__________
legal	__________	cooked	__________
regular	__________	probable	__________
lucky	__________	correct	__________

Now use one of the words you have made in its correct form to complete the sentences below.

1 I'm afraid you have __________ this word: there are two *C*s and two *M*s in *accommodation*.
2 Young people like to feel that they are __________ enough to make their own decisions without consulting their parents.
3 This answer is __________ : 277 minus 135 is not 152.
4 My brother's arrival on Monday was completely __________ as he was supposed to be coming on Tuesday.
5 In some countries the number 13 is __________ .
6 I wish you wouldn't __________ with everything I say!
7 Some people say that new radio presenter is funny but I think he talks a lot of __________ .
8 Doctors work very __________ hours so you never know when they are going to be at home.
9 Years ago people thought it would be __________ to fly to the moon!
10 Did you know that it was __________ to park on double yellow lines in this country?

G Writing

Look at the cross-section of the plans an architect has drawn up for you. Write to a friend describing the house you are going to have built.

Don't forget to:
- give an overall picture of the house.
- give particular details of the house, e.g. number of floors
- say what you feel about the house.

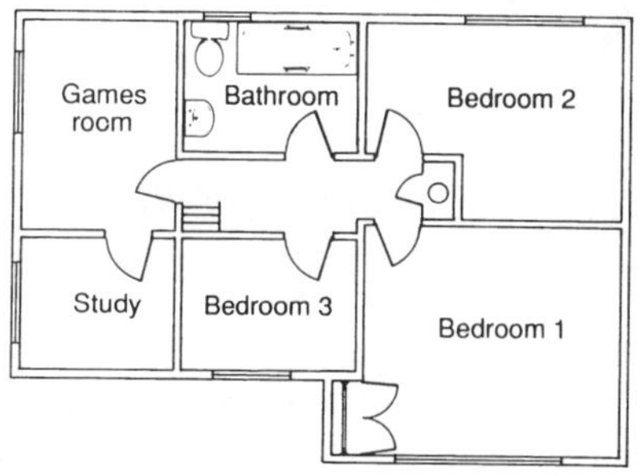

FIRST FLOOR

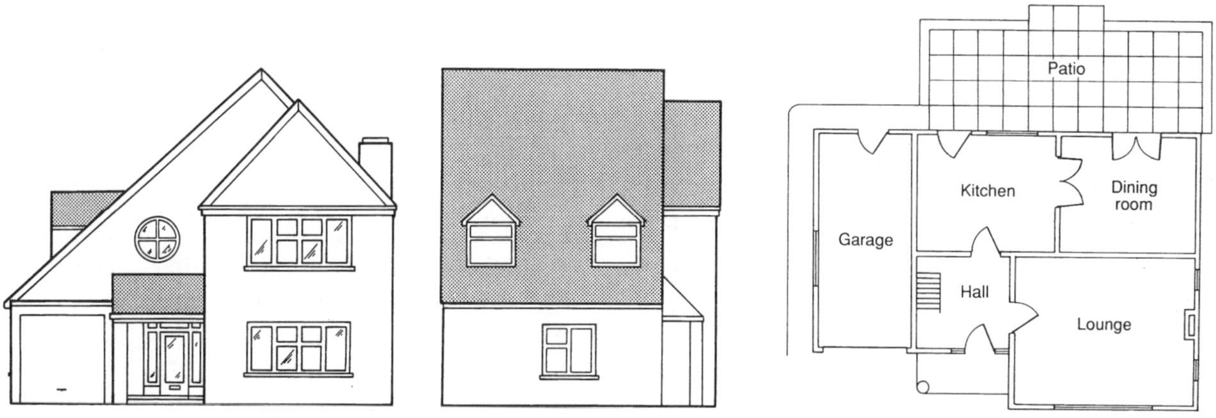

FRONT ELEVATION

SIDE ELEVATION

GROUND FLOOR

H Language study 2

Rewrite sentences 1–6 using *what*.

Examples:
You're saying something. I can't make out what.
I can't make out what you're saying.

You believe something. It is not necessarily true.
What you believe is not necessarily true.

1 You said something. It was untrue.

____

2 She said something. Did it upset you?

____

3 I ought to do something. I haven't thought about it.

____

4 They suggested something. It was very practical.

____

5 They did something to you. Was it terrible?

____

6 Something made him do it. I don't understand it.

____

7 They told him something. It was very interesting.

____

8 He told me something. I'll never be able to forget it.

____

UNIT 14

A Reading

Read the article about a mother and her son's memories. Five paragraphs have been removed from the article. Choose from paragraphs A–F the one which fits each gap (1–4). There is one extra paragraph which you do not need. There is an example at the beginning (0).

I remember once taking my three-year-old son Daniel, who remembers the incident very well too, to stay with my mother for two days, not without some misgivings for I knew that my mother had been a great one for discipline and attached great importance to good manners. On the other hand she was very fond of Daniel, and he of her, because when she came to stay with us she liked to read him stories.

0 *C*

When I phoned my mother to ask what had happened, she told me that Daniel had cried when she tried to explain to him at table that a well-brought-up little boy mustn't go ahead and help himself without saying 'please' and 'thank you'. My mother felt that I spoilt Daniel and that I was teaching him very bad manners.

1 ___

She didn't realize that she was threatening the child with a withdrawal of love if he didn't obey. And above all she didn't realize, as she hadn't in my own case, that she was sacrificing the child's soul to empty conventions just as had been done to her sixty years earlier.

2 ___

The story was perfectly simple: the dessert was Daniel's favourite, chocolate soufflé. When he had finished the helping he had been given, he picked up the serving spoon and reached out to help himself to some more.

3 ___

At this point Daniel threw down the spoon and refused to eat any more, although my mother urged him to: he said he wasn't hungry anymore and wanted to go home.

4 ___

My mother said nothing in reply, then, after a while he asked: 'Why did you do that? I know how to help myself.' 'Yes,' said my mother, 'but you must first ask whether you may.' 'Why?' asked Daniel. 'Because you must learn good manners.' 'What for?' asked Daniel. 'Because one needs them,' replied my mother. Daniel then said quite calmly: '*I* don't need them. With Mummy I can eat when I'm hungry!'

A She felt obliged to correct this so that later on the child wouldn't annoy people and be treated with contempt and dislike, instead of love, by those around him. She was convinced she was trying to help him and wasn't aware that she was under a compulsion originating in her childhood fear.

B This child is allowed to defend himself, to show his anger, when his natural gesture is impeded and he is given a reason that he doesn't understand, can't understand, and shouldn't understand, because it is senseless and really only comprehensible in terms of his grandmother's history.

C However, when I picked him up after his stay, he said to me in the car: 'I don't want to stay with Grandma any more.' I could hardly believe my ears. His comment completely took me by surprise. I hesitantly asked him why, and he replied: 'She hurt me.'

D But Daniel realized it. He couldn't have put it into words, not in the way that I do now, but he expressed it in the way that was possible to *him*, as I found out from the exact description of the facts that gradually developed from my mother's account.

E He always does this at home, taking great pride in his independence. But now my mother held him back, gently placing her hand, as she told me, on his and saying: 'You must first ask whether you may have some and whether there is enough for others.' 'Where are the others?' asked Daniel, who by now was upset.

F My mother tried to calm him, but he then threw a real tantrum. These tantrums, which he very rarely had, never lasted long and, after a few minutes his rage was spent. He said: 'You hurt me, I don't like you. I want to go to Mummy.'

B Language study 1

Match the sentences on the left with the meanings they express on the right. Draw lines between the pairs.

I remembered to post the letter.	I didn't post the letter.
I remember posting the letter.	I told you to post the letter.
I remember you posting the letter	I recall that you posted the letter.
I reminded you to post the letter.	I didn't forget to post the letter.
I forgot to post the letter.	I posted the letter, but I don't recall it.
I can't remember posting the letter.	I recall that I posted the letter.

Now complete the sentences in the letter below using the words in brackets in their correct form and supplying any missing words. There is an example at the beginning (0).

Dear Mary,

I can't apologise enough for not remembering (0) _to contact_ (contact) you on your birthday. Mother did remind me (1)__________(buy) you a birthday card and a present when I went shopping. Well, I remembered (2)__________(buy) a card but I forgot (3)__________(get) a present. I actually looked for one, but I saw a pair of shoes and bought them instead! When I got home, I found that I had some guests. I couldn't remember (4)__________(invite) them to lunch, probably because I'd forgotten (5)__________(write) the arrangement down in my diary. Anyway, what with the guests and everything, your birthday went clean out of my mind. I'm really sorry I didn't remember (6)__________(buy) you a present. Will you have lunch with me next week instead? You needn't remind me (7)__________(turn up)! I promise I won't forget (8)__________(meet) you!

Love,

Vera

C Writing

Now write a few sentences describing your very first memory when you were a child.

D Vocabulary 1

Complete the following table where appropriate:

Noun	Verb	Adjective
injury	__________	__________
harm	__________	__________
damage	__________	__________
ruin	__________	__________
	hurt	__________
	spoil	__________

Now use the most suitable word from the table, in the correct form, to complete the sentences below.

1 The __________ motorist was taken to hospital.

2 The man was suffering from severe __________ .

3 The soldiers captured the terrorists without __________ the hostages.

4 Cigarette smoking can __________ your health.

5 It's only an injection! The needle won't __________ you!

6 You've __________ the surprise by telling him!

7 I know what you say is true, but it still __________ my feelings.

8 The fire caused extensive __________ to the ground floor.

9 Adding the extra salt was a mistake. It __________ the taste of the soup.

10 You'll come to no __________ if you follow my instructions carefully.

11 His risky investments led to financial __________ .

12 What she said in her letter was enough to __________ my day.

E Use of English

Read the text. If a line is correct, put a tick (✓). If a line has an unnecessary word, underline it. There are two examples at the beginning (0) and (00).

0 Alex Thompson, a law student, was knocked off his ✓
00 motorbike by a car in the August, 1994, near Reading.
1 'All of a sudden I was floating above the scene of the
2 accident looking down.' Then Alex began to be pulled
3 down a dark tunnel of which he found breathtaking. 'It
4 made fairground rides seem quite as tame!' Standing at
5 the mouth of the tunnel was a man, whom Alex felt was
6 an old friend. 'I laughed when I reached to him and
7 I said him, 'I'm really glad that's over.' It was
8 all such a relief, like if waking up from a
9 nightmare!' He was shown in a beautiful garden,
10 and he saw some people in the distance whom he
11 recognized as if his dead relatives and friends. Then
12 he was told that he had ever to go back to finish his
13 'job' on earth. 'I begged not to have got to go. But
14 the man said I had to. Then, all suddenly I zipped
15 back down the tunnel, and I woke me up with back, leg
and head injuries.'

F Language study 2

Match the phrases on the left with the meanings they express on the right. Draw lines between the pairs.

must have done	something you ought to have done but didn't do
should have done	something you could possibly have done
might have done	something you are reasonably certain did happen

Now rewrite the following sentences using *must/should/might have (done)*.

Example:
I'm sorry I wasn't at home when you phoned. I know I promised to be.
I should have been at home when you phoned.

1 Perhaps I was asleep when you called because I didn't hear the phone.

2 I'm sure I was in the bath when the phone rang.

3 It would have been better if you had tried ringing again.

4 Perhaps you would have caught me later on in the evening.

5 I'm sure you knew I was expecting your call.

6 John wasn't at home either. Perhaps he went to the cinema.

7 I'm certain he stayed out late because he sounded very tired this morning.

8 It would have been better if he had gone out on Saturday instead.

G Vocabulary 2

Make word combinations, with hyphens, to match the phrases below.

Example:
A contract which lasts for two years
A two-year contract

> ***Remember:*** there is no *-s* at the end of *year* when it is used in a word combination like this.

1 A street in which traffic can travel only one way

2 A family with only one parent

3 A jug which holds two litres

4 A holiday which lasts two weeks

5 A suit consisting of three pieces

6 A lesson which lasts fifty minutes

7 A word consisting of three letters

8 A saloon car with four doors

9 A working week of five days

10 An interval of five minutes

H Writing

Look at the map of York and answer the question below.

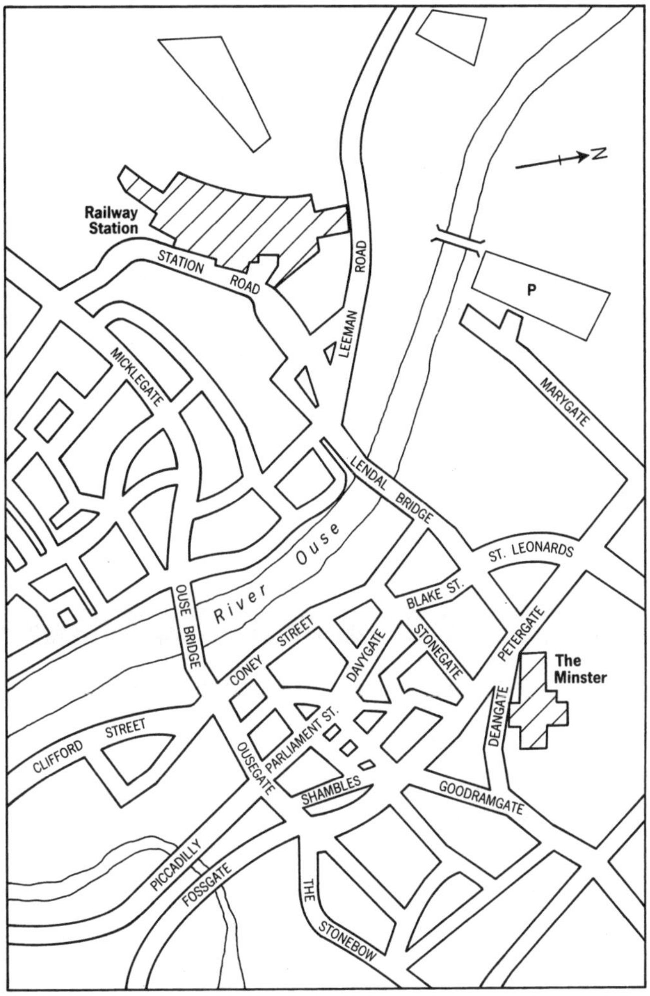

A friend of yours is coming to York, where you live, for your birthday. You are going to meet outside the Minster and then go somewhere for supper. Afterwards you will go to a disco in Piccadilly. Write a note to your friend in the space provided explaining how to get to the Minster from the station on foot, and then explain how to get from the Minster to Piccadilly in case your friend is late and misses you.

UNIT 15

A Reading

Read the text and choose the best answer in 1–6.

Jules is now in his sixties, and is one of the many homeless people who live on the streets; he buys a newspaper most days. Today, with his fellow tramps, he reads about yesterday's student demonstrations.

Like many of the tramps who live under the bridges in Paris, Jules was not always so poor. A long time ago he was in the Navy, and like many who have been to sea for a long time, he has stayed slim and fit. Despite the strict organization on board ship, he loved the life, and had the opportunity to see many countries. He visited Poland and Russia; in South Africa he realized what he valued in each country was the people he met. He was always astonished and delighted by the ways in which the people he met differed from one country to another. Some day, he hopes, everyone will see the world as he does.

After many happy years in the Navy, he had to retire. The good things in life always come to an end. His mother and father had long since died and he'd lost touch with his other relatives. He came to Paris and became an industrial designer. He was happy, although it wasn't the same as the sea. He never wanted to get married and have children.

And then there was the period of darkness. He smiles sadly. He shrugs his shoulders and looks at his hands. There are tears in the corners of his eyes. This is something that he cannot bring himself to talk about. 'It all went wrong,' he whispers.

He was silent for a minute, then recovered. He began to talk more loudly. 'Look at me now – it makes me angry. And what about the President? He's been in power for years, and look what he's done for us. Nothing! I'm still out on the streets and I live the life of a dog.'

1 It would appear that Jules
   A takes an interest in important events.
   B has organized a protest recently.
   C has no contact with other homeless people.
   D is not as poor as he used to be.

2 When Jules was in the Navy, he
   A only visited three countries.
   B enjoyed the strict life on board ship.
   C liked meeting people from different countries.
   D was very well paid for the job he did.

3 Jules changed his job because he
   A was too old to stay in the Navy.
   B wanted to start a family.
   C wanted to be near his relatives in Paris.
   D did not enjoy the work any more.

4 Jules lost his job and became a tramp because
   A of reasons he does not want to discuss.
   B he did not have any family.
   C of the death of his parents.
   D he was tired of doing a normal job.

5 The text states that Jules thinks the President
   A has not had enough time to change things.
   B should not allow homeless people to stay on the streets.
   C should increase pensions for old people
   D should have done more to help people like him.

6 The writer's attitude towards Jules is
   A critical.
   B unfriendly.
   C uncaring.
   D sympathetic.

B Vocabulary 1

Find a word from the text that means:

1 without a place to live ________

2 poor people who live on the streets ________

3 meetings or protest marches ________

4 thin ________

5 healthy, in good condition ________

6 severe, tough ________

7 had a high opinion of something ________

8 speaks very quietly ________

C Vocabulary 2

Fill in the spaces with one of these words connected with law.

fined	prosecution	court
jury	lawyer	cross-examined
witnesses	evidence	accused
defence	trial	verdict
guilty	sentenced	judge

The (1)__________ of Mr Arthur Sanderson , who has been (2)__________ of stealing large sums of money from his company, opened at the High Court last week. On the first day, the lawyer for the (3)__________ said that he would prove that Sanderson had stolen the money. He questioned a number of (4)__________, who explained that they had heard Sanderson talking about stealing the money. Later on, the (5)__________ for the (6)__________ had a chance to explain Sanderson's side of the story. He (7)__________ the witnesses, and tried to show that the (8)__________ that they had given was not true. On the final day, the (9)__________ went over the main facts of the case, and asked the twelve members of the (10)__________ to leave the (11)__________ and decide on a (12)__________. When they came back in, they said they had found Sanderson (13)__________ of all the charges against him. The judge (14)__________ him to two years in prison, and she also (15)__________ him £100,000.

D Language study 1

Rewrite these sentences using the word in bold.

1 Susan hasn't phoned me for weeks.

last

It's ______________ me.

2 I last smoked three months ago.

for

I ______________ months.

3 I haven't seen Henry since 1994.

time

The last ______________ in 1994.

4 It's more than six months since I went to the dentist.

for

I haven't ______________ more than six months.

5 I haven't watched TV for ages, so I'm not sure what's happened in the story.

ago

The last time I ______________ , so I'm not sure what's happened in the story.

6 Alan's cat died three years ago.

was

It ______________ Alan's cat died.

7 When was the last time you had a check-up?

long

How ______________ had a check-up?

8 It's been ages since I went to the cinema.

for

I haven't ______________ ages.

E Language study 2

Give your own answers to the following questions.

Examples:
When did you last go to hospital?
I haven't been to hospital for nearly six years.
It's been six years since I last went to hospital.
The last time I went to hospital was six years ago.

1 When was the last time you had a row with someone in your family?

____

2 When was the last time you went on holiday?

____

3 When was the last time you took an exam?

____

4 When was the last time you were given a present?

____

5 When was the last time you had breakfast in bed?

____

6 When was the last time you took any exercise?

____

7 When was the last time you made someone really angry?

____

8 When was the last time you went out for a meal?

____

F Language study 3

Write down a suggestion you might make in the following situations.

Examples:

Emma is feeling a bit bored.

Why don't you ask Larry round? OR

Let's go out for the evening. OR

What about going out for the evening? OR

Wouldn't it be a good idea to go out?

1 You're shopping with Laura and she hasn't got enough cash to buy what she wants. (Nor have you.)

Why ______________________________

______________________________?

2 Jack is trying to get in touch with Peter, but hasn't got his phone number or address.

Wouldn't ______________________________

______________________________?

3 You and Lucy want something to eat, but there's nothing in the house.

Let's ______________________________

______________________________?

4 Roddy needs to visit some relatives in London, but his car has broken down.

What ______________________________

______________________________?

5 You and David and a few other friends are wondering what to do this evening.

Why ______________________________

______________________________?

G Language study 4

Now report the five suggestions you made in F.

Example:

Why don't you ask Larry round?
I suggested to Emma that she should invite Larry round.
Let's go out for the evening.
I suggested going out for the evening.

1 ______________________________

2 ______________________________

3 ______________________________

4 ______________________________

5 ______________________________

H Vocabulary 3

Complete the sentences with one of the words below.

cost value price expense worth

1 Although they look like diamonds, the stones have no real ________ .

2 When business people take clients out to lunch, they don't pay themselves – the bill goes on their ________ account.

3 The ________ of living in Switzerland is much higher than it is in Spain.

4 In the furniture shop they gave me their latest ________ list, so now I know what everything costs.

5 The shop assistant didn't know how much the sweater was because the ________ tag was missing.

6 It's not ________ repairing those old shoes. It'd be much better just to get some new ones.

7 The ________ of travelling by train has increased considerably over the last few years.

8 It was when I really needed her help, and she offered it, that I realized the true ________ of her friendship.

I Language study 5

Rewrite these sentences using the word in bold.

1 'Now where have I put the keys?' Emma asked herself.

wondered

Emma ________________ the keys.

2 'You're not paying attention,' my instructor said.

criticized

My instructor ________________ paying attention.

3 'Please, please don't drive the motorbike too fast,' Jake's mother said.

urged

Jake's mother ________________ the motorbike too fast.

4 'You're a liar!' Annabel said to her husband.

of

Annabel ________________ to her.

5 The guide said to us: 'Don't go into the jungle – it's dangerous.'

warned

The guide ________________ into the jungle.

6 'If I were you, I'd see a lawyer,' Laura said to me.

should

Laura suggested ________________ a lawyer.

7 In court, the lawyer said I was a thief.

accused

In court the lawyer ________________ a thief.

8 'Lets go out for a meal,' Jane said to me.

suggested

Jane ________________ a meal.

J Use of English

Read the text about Kevin Rogers and decide which word, A, B, C or D, best fits each space. There is an example at the beginning (0).

While I was (0)___*in*___ prison, I spent a lot of time (1)_____ about what had gone wrong. Obviously the Contessa and I had (2)_____ a mistake somewhere, but we had taken a lot of trouble to (3)_____ to it that no one would catch us. I (4)_____ a bad time in prison, but while I was there, I (5)_____ a decision that I would find Pilar again when I got out and we would spend the rest of our lives together.

Just before I was released, I had a visitor. It was my lawyer. He said he just wanted to (6)_____ a word with me about Pilar. I hoped he would tell me where she was, but he (7)_____ me to stop looking for her and (8)_____ me that it would not do me any good. I explained to him that I had (9)_____ a promise to Pilar that I would never forget her.

It was then that he told me something that finally allowed me to (10)_____ through her. The police had told him that it had been Pilar who had betrayed me. We (11)_____ an argument, and of course I (12)_____ him of (13)_____ it all up, but somehow I knew that he was telling the truth.

A few days later I was released. I realized that I had (14)_____ a terrible mess of my life. I started drinking, and (15)_____ on drinking until I had lost everything, and ended up on the streets. It took me years to recover.

0	A at	B into	C in	D to
1	A inquiring	B wondering	C demanding	D regarding
2	A done	B made	C had	D taken
3	A watch	B look	C see	D notice
4	A had	B passed	C spent	D did
5	A made	B did	C held	D found
6	A speak	B have	C give	D say
7	A urged	B suggested	C indicated	D argued
8	A avoided	B warned	C noticed	D prevented
9	A done	B had	C made	D taken
10	A look	B see	C watch	D notice
11	A made	B took	C had	D did
12	A claimed	B charged	C blamed	D accused
13	A doing	B saying	C inventing	D making
14	A done	B taken	C made	D had
15	A stayed	B kept	C continued	D remained

PROGRESS TEST 3

A Vocabulary cloze

Decide which word, A, B, C or D, best fits each space. There is an example at the beginning (0).

THE PERFECT PARTNER

A long and happy (0) *marriage* is something that many people wish for, but finding the right partner is (1)______ more difficult than you might imagine. A friend of mine, Susan, had not been very successful in her (2)______ to find the perfect partner, and she was beginning to lose heart and feel rather (3)______ . One day she happened to hear someone (4)______ about a computer dating agency which could help you to find the ideal partner. Susan immediately (5)______ an appointment to see someone at the agency, then waited to see (6)______ would happen. The agency arranged a meeting with a 'suitable' partner at the local railway station a week later, although I (7)______ her not to go. My friend arrived a few minutes (8)______ but could see no one who matched the (9)______ of the man in the photograph she had been sent. She (10)______ a man waiting under the station clock and (11)______ a bunch of flowers, but there was no one (12)______ around. Suddenly the man started chatting to her and, after a while, asked her if she would (13)______ to go and have a coffee. Not (14)______ much later did they come to the conclusion that they had both been waiting for each other! When they had both (15)______ from the shock, they decided that the computer had been right after all!

0 A honeymoon B wedding C marriage D engagement
1 A so B much C too D lot
2 A fight B duty C work D attempt
3 A depressed B ashamed C embarrassed D bored
4 A mentioning B telling C talking D relating
5 A did B had C set D made
6 A that B what C which D who
7 A advised B urged C suggested D whispered
8 A after B since C ago D early
9 A look B appearance C gesture D manner
10 A realized B considered C noticed D respected
11 A fetching B wearing C carrying D holding
12 A more B other C extra D else
13 A want B desire C like D need
14 A until B when C then D after
15 A returned B recovered C reviewed D realized

B Open cloze

Think of ONE word which best fits each space. There is an example at the beginning (0).

IMPROVE YOUR MEMORY

Teachers have often used memory tests to assess the intelligence (0) *of* their students. But having a good memory often has little to (1)________ with intelligence. Studies have shown not only that some people (2)________ below average intelligence have exceptional memories, but (3)________ that some highly intelligent people have poor memories. A good memory is more often the result of using techniques that can (4)________ learned, and many of the books that have (5)________ written on the subject encourage people to use similar methods. One of (6)________ is to make up short sentences or rhymes which can help you remember (7)________ you need to know by heart. (8)________ example, the first letters of the words in the sentence 'Richard of York gained battles in vain' are ROYGBIV; these (9)________ the colours of the rainbow – red, orange, yellow, and (10)________ on. Another technique involves linking the sounds (11)________ words with images, which can be particularly effective when learning new words. The learner needs (12)________ create an image to help to remember the word. By using techniques (13)________ this, many learners find it a lot easier (14)________ they had expected to keep (15)________ learning new vocabulary.

C Key word transformations

Rewrite the sentences using the word in bold.

1 She sprained her ankle and broke her leg.
only
Not __________________ her ankle but she broke her leg as well.

2 Someone's making new curtains for me.
made
I'm __________________ for me.

3 Don't you think this is the most boring film you have ever seen?
such
Have you __________________ film before?

4 People say Chinese food is the best in the world.
said
Chinese food __________________ the best in the world.

5 It's three weeks since I saw Robin.
for
I __________________ three weeks.

6 'Don't you think you should buy a small car?' Jack said to me.
suggested
Jack __________________ buy a small car.

7 'Why don't we play tennis?' Mary said to me.
suggested
Mary __________________ tennis.

8 How did you persuade Thomas to lend you the money?
talk
How did you __________________ you the money?

9 'Don't stop on the double yellow line!' the policeman told us.
warned
The policeman __________________ on the double yellow line.

10 I can never compensate for what I have done.
make
How can I __________________ what I have done?

D Error correction

In the following text, some lines contain a mistake. Tick the lines that are correct and underline the words that you do not need. There are two examples at the beginning (0) and (00).

LIFE AT THE TOP

0 Scully was the sort of man who should have been a success in life. ✓
00 If he had not been brought it up in one of the roughest parts of the
1 city, he might have stood a chance. But the luck plays a big part in
2 our lives, and Scully was destined to become himself one of the
3 best-known and most richest criminals of all time. He had begun his
4 working life to doing odd jobs in a factory but he quickly made his way
5 up the ladder of success and, aged only 26, was one of the most
6 successful property developers who he operated in the city. People
7 like as Scully make a lot of friends and even more enemies. His business
8 deals were known to be illegal but nobody could prove, or perhaps had the
9 courage to try and prove, just how to illegal they were. He lived
10 a life of luxury. He was a handsome man and spent a great deal of time
11 in having holidays in the sun. He was always surrounded by beautiful
12 women. Unfortunately, he became over-confident and started taking
13 foolish risks of which naturally ended in disaster. As evidence against
14 him grew, he fled the country and was eventually picked him up on a
15 luxury yacht in the Mediterranean. He is now serving a 10-year sentence
for fraud!

UNIT 16

A Reading

Read the article about robots. Choose the most suitable heading from the list A–I for each part of the article (1–7). There is one heading which you do not need. There is an example at the beginning (0).

0 *F*

The most sophisticated Japanese robots, which have vision systems and work at very high speeds, are still based on American designs. Studies of robots, particularly computer control software, are considered to be generally less advanced in Japan than in America or Europe.

1 ____

Although industrial robots were originally developed as devices for simply handling objects, today their commonest uses are for more skilled work like welding, spray painting and assembling components.

2 ____

In Britain, robot sales appropriately peaked in 1984, but have been declining ever since. This is partly because British wage rates are too low to make robots financially attractive and partly because engineers now have more experience with robots and are more aware of the difficulties of introducing them effectively.

3 ____

It has been calculated that a robot uses on average about 100 times more energy than a human to do an equivalent job.

4 ____

It is estimated that 20% of all comic book heroes in Japan are robots. This is an enormous number because comics are so popular that they make up a third of all material published in Japan.

5 ____

Until recently a 50Kg robot arm with the same reach as a human could only lift 1Kg. The latest 20Kg robots can lift 2Kg, but this is still no match for a human arm which weighs about 5Kg and can lift 50Kg.

6 ____

The reliability of robots is measured in their M.T.B.F. or mean time between failures. This has risen from about 250 hours in the mid 70s to about 10,000 hours today (equivalent to working 18 hours a day for two years). One way robot manufacturers have increased reliability is to test every single component they buy, instead of the normal procedure of just testing a small sample.

7 ____

The biggest single benefit of introducing robots claimed by Japanese companies is that they increase quality control. Once programmed, their output is more accurate and consistent than humans, who can get tired and bored.

A FALLING DEMAND
B ROBOT STARS
C DEPENDABILITY
D INEFFICIENCY
E NEAR PERFECTION
F RESEARCH
G CHANGING ROLES
H HIDDEN DANGER
I MUSCLE POWER

B Vocabulary 1

Match the words on the left with the words of a similar meaning on the right. Draw lines between the pairs.

range	extraordinary
tasks	highly-developed
expert	mend
unusual	answer
repair	a little
slightly	identify
sophisticated	assortment
equivalent	corresponding
recognize	jobs
respond	specialist

Now use one of the words from the left-hand column, in its correct form, to complete the sentences below.

1 My cassette recorder is broken. I'll have to get it __________ .

2 One of the many __________ a computer can perform is keeping your accounts.

3 Some of the expensive machines are much more __________ and capable of remembering more data.

4 We have a wide __________ of models in stock.

5 What is __________ to US$2 in pounds sterling?

6 I'm afraid you'll have to speak up. He's __________ deaf.

7 According to __________, the earth's temperature will rise considerably in the future.

8 I didn't __________ him at first, as he had grown a beard.

9 Her illness must be very serious. She is not __________ to the treatment at all.

10 What was __________ was that she had one brown eye and one green eye.

C Language study 1

Look at the list of predictions for the future and complete the sentences saying what *will* happen in, or *will/may* have happened by, the years given.

Examples: 2000/2002
In 2000 there will be a dramatic rise in the world population.
By the year 2002 the world population will have risen dramatically.

PREDICTIONS FOR THE FUTURE

2000	Dramatic rise in world population
2005	Cars banned from all city centres
2010	People settle on the moon
2015	Animals discovered on other planets
2020	World peace achieved
2025	Food supplies run out
2030	War with beings on other planets occurs

---

1 ... 2005/2006 ....
2 ... 2010/2011 ....
3 ... 2015/2016 ....
4 ... 2020/2023 ....
5 ... 2025/2027 ....
6 ... 2030/2032 ....

Which of these predictions do you think won't have happened by the times above?

D Phrasal verbs

Fill the spaces with the correct form of one of these phrasal verbs.

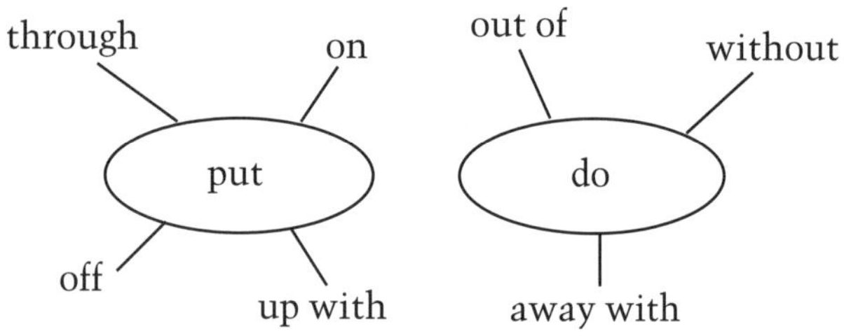

1 There are no vegetables in the fridge so we'll just have to ______ them.

2 ______ your bathing costume and we'll go for a swim.

3 In most Western countries they have ______ capital punishment.

4 I know the noise is dreadful but we'll have to ______ it until the builders have finished.

5 When his uncle died, some distant relatives tried to ______ him ______ his inheritance.

6 I'll try to ______ you ______ to the managing director in a minute.

7 Never ______ until tomorrow what you can do today!

8 I'm not going to ______ your rudeness any longer! I'm leaving!

9 I can't ______ going to the doctor any longer. This pain is getting worse.

10 Have you any sugar? I can't ______ a spoonful in my coffee.

E Language study 2

Rephrase the statements in different ways using *seem to be (doing)* or *act as if* in their correct form.

Example: 'I think Peter's ill.'
Peter seems to be ill.
Peter is acting as if he's ill.

1 I have the impression that Susie's upset.
2 The manager is acting strangely today. He could be worried about something.
3 I don't think you understand a word I'm saying!
4 It appears that the children have not studied this subject before.
5 I think John knew exactly what I was talking about.
6 I have the impression that people are not very optimistic about the future.

F Vocabulary 2

These words are often confused. Can you put the appropriate word into the sentences below? In some cases more than one word may be correct.

untrue	artificial
false	man-made
wrong	fake
lying	imitation
dishonest	synthetic

1 I bought a lovely pair of cheap shoes in ______ leather.

2 He said he was a doctor but he was a ______.

3 A lot of material nowadays consists of ______ fibres.

4 You are ______. 65 and 75 do not make 155.

5 He says he's been working late but I think he's ______.

6 A(n) ______ accusation was made against him.

7 Stealing is ______.

8 If someone is finding difficulty in breathing, ______ respiration can be given.

9 I can no longer tell if what he says is true or ______.

10 ______ fur is very popular with animal lovers.

G Writing

Write four short paragraphs giving two or three pieces of advice in each paragraph to a friend who is about to do these things:

1 travel abroad
2 take a speaking test in a foreign language
3 learn to drive a car
4 live in a bed-sitter

Use some of these expressions to help you:

If I were you, I'd...

You ought to ...

Whatever you do, don't ... in case / unless ...

It's well worth ...ing ...

I don't think you should ...

It's best not to ....

1 ______________________________

____

____

____

____

2 ______________________________

____

____

____

____

3 ______________________________

____

____

____

____

4 ______________________________

____

____

____

____

H Language study 3

Rewrite the sentences using the word in bold.

Example:
The instructions are so easy that even a child can understand them.
enough
The instructions are *easy enough for even* a child to understand.

1 The exercise is so difficult that the students can't do it.

too

The exercise is ________________ to do.

2 The car is so cheap that Jim could actually buy it!

enough

The car is ________________ buy.

3 The dress is so tight that Sally can't get into it.

too

The dress is ________________ get into.

4 The water is so warm that the children can go for a swim.

enough

The water is ________________ to go for a swim.

5 The table is so small that the family can't all fit around it.

too

The table is ________________ to fit around.

6 The room is so big that the students could hold a party in it.

enough

The room is ________________ to hold a party in.

UNIT 17

A Reading

Read the text and choose the best answer in 1–6.

FIRE-FIGHTING

How to fight a fire

Anyone who uses fire-extinguishers should know a few basic facts about how to make them work. This leaflet will tell you the most important things to remember if you have to put a fire out.

Water extinguishers

You can put most fires out with water extinguishers. However, you should not use water extinguishers if the fire involves electrical equipment or if it has been started by flammable liquids such as petrol or paraffin.

As in all fires, make sure that the wind is behind you – if you do this, the smoke will blow away from you. Point the jet of water at the bottom of the fire and move it slowly higher.

Remember that you should only use extinguishers for small fires. If there is any danger of the fire spreading to anything that can explode – a gas cylinder for example – you should not try to put the fire out yourself. Instead, leave the building immediately and call the fire brigade.

Foam extinguishers

You can use a foam extinguisher for fires caused by burning liquids such as petrol. Never point the jet directly into the liquid itself, as this may make it splash and spread the fire. Instead, try and point the extinguisher up into the air so that the foam goes up and falls on top of the burning liquid.

Whatever the kind of fire, do not stand up straight – if you can stay down, this will help you to avoid the smoke, and you may be able to get closer to the fire. Get out of the building at once if you think your escape route might be cut off by smoke or fire.

Carbon Dioxide extinguishers

Some fire extinguishers are filled with a gas called carbon dioxide. You can use these to put out fires which have been caused either by electrical equipment or flammable liquids. If the fire has been caused by electrical equipment, switch the equipment off and point the extinguisher straight at the fire. If the fire has been caused by a liquid like petrol, point the extinguisher at the nearest edge of the fire, and move it from side to side.

Remember, never stay in a building if it is dangerous to do so, or if the fire grows beyond your control. Make sure you are standing near an exit in case this happens.

1 Water extinguishers can be used
A on the majority of small fires.
B unless the wind is blowing the wrong way.
C on fires that involve liquids like petrol.
D to put out fires in electrical equipment.

2 According to the text, you should leave a burning building
A as soon as the fire alarm goes off.
B as soon as you discover a fire.
C if the smoke is blowing towards you.
D if there is a risk of something blowing up.

3 If you use a foam extinguisher, you need to
A aim it at the centre of the liquid that is burning.
B try and cover the liquid with the foam.
C aim it at the edge of the liquid.
D get as close to the fire as possible.

4 You should not stand up to fight a fire
A if the fire involves electrical equipment.
B under any circumstances.
C because this will allow you to keep a safe distance.
D because extinguishers are heavy to carry.

5 You should aim the gas from a carbon dioxide extinguisher
A at the top of a fire involving electrical equipment.
B straight into a fire involving burning liquid.
C into the middle of a fire involving electrical equipment.
D so that it lands on top of the burning liquid.

6 The overall purpose of the text is to
A persuade people to buy an extinguisher.
B explain how fire extinguishers work.
C tell people how to use extinguishers.
D train professional fire-fighters.

B Vocabulary

Look at the list of natural disasters and group them under the headings of Earth, Wind, Fire and Water. Some may come under more than one heading. Use your dictionary to help you.

landslide	earthquake	flood	hurricane
avalanche	tidal wave	sandstorm	drought
eruption	forest fire	blizzard	typhoon

Earth	Wind	Fire	Water

Now read these extracts from descriptions of natural disasters. Write down the name of the disaster being described.

1 ...and suddenly the mountain seemed to explode, sending flames and rocks into the air ...

____

2 ...the large mass of ice and snow crashed down the side of the mountain, burying everything ...

____

3 ...the wind lashed the buildings, tearing the roofs of houses and uprooting trees ...

____

4 ...as the wind and snow increased, it became impossible to see more than a few metres ahead ...

____

5 ...there had been no rain for six months, and the rivers had run dry; the animals were dying ...

____

6 ...the rivers broke their banks and water poured into the fields ...

____

C Language study 1

Fill the spaces with *could, couldn't* or an appropriate form of *managed to*.

> ***Remember:*** *managed to* means *tried and succeeded.*

When I was at school, I was good at languages, and (1)__________(I/speak) French and German quite well. (2)__________(I/even/pass) my exams, and I got quite good grades. But what surprised me was that when I went to Germany for the first time, (3)__________(I/understand) a word – it was as if they were speaking a completely different language from the one I had learned. On the whole (4)__________(I/speak) quite well but it was a long time before (5)__________(I/have) my first real conversation.

D Language study 2

Read the sentences A–H. Then say which sentence with *must* from 1–8 could be used to continue it.

Example: *A 6*

A *There's no answer from her phone.*
B You've been staying late at the office for weeks.
C Your exam results are going to be terrible.
D Tell your brother his room is terribly untidy.
E Actually, Jack's room isn't in a mess.
F This is a secret between you and me.
G His breath smelled of cigarettes.
H This flowerpot feels very light.

1 He must have been smoking.
2 You must work harder.
3 He must clear it up.
4 It must be made of plastic.
5 He must have cleared it up this morning.
6 *She must be out.*
7 You must have a lot of work to do.
8 You mustn't tell anyone.

Now rewrite the following sentences using the word in bold.

1 It's important that someone meets Mr Andrews at the airport.
must
Mr Andrews __________ at the airport.

2 The thief almost certainly came in through the window.
come
The thief __________ through the window.

3 I'm sure you were driving too fast.
been
You __________ too fast.

4 It's essential that your homework gets done before you go out.
must
You __________ before you go out.

5 I'm sure someone stole his bike while we were in the shop.
have
His bike __________ while we were in the shop.

6 If he's not in the office, then I'm sure he's working at home.
must
If he's not in the office, __________ at home.

E Use of English 1

Read the text. If a line is correct, put a tick (✓). If a line has an unnecessary word, underline it. There are two examples at the beginning (0) and (00).

0 The authorities in Bangladesh are doing their best for ✓
00 the victims of the floods which have been covered
1 many of low-lying coastal villages. The floods were
2 caused by a combination of very high spring tides and
3 too heavy rainfall in the mountains, which, according to
4 government sources, could not to have been predicted.
5 The government has called in the army to the affected
6 areas, and they are handing out a food to the people
7 who could have managed to get away from the flood
8 by moving to more higher ground. The authorities
9 estimate that there are must be several thousand
10 people are in need of urgent medical attention.
11 The Red Cross insists that the United Nations must
12 have provide more emergency aid for the affected
13 area. As a result of the tragedy, the planned
14 independence celebrations they have been called off,
15 and the Prime Minister has been cancelled his visit
to the USA.

F Use of English 2

Read the text and decide which word, A, B, C or D, best fits each space. There is an example at the beginning (0).

CLIMBER WHO 'DIED' IN MONT BLANC STORM IS BROUGHT BACK TO LIFE

A climber whose heart had stopped beating in a snowstorm on Mont Blanc was (0) *revived* by French doctors during a five-hour operation yesterday. Alan Haywood, 41, had set off with three friends on Saturday to climb Mont Blanc. Early on Sunday morning the (1)_____ had set off for the summit, and although the skies were (2)_____ at first, it soon began to snow heavily. As the storm got worse, they (3)_____ see where they were going. They had no (4)_____ but to dig a hole in the snow to keep the (5)_____ in and wait for the storm to pass. They were (6)_____ for 24 hours. During the night, Mr Haywood's body temperature began to fall, and when it dropped to below 25°C, his heart stopped beating. His friends feared the worst and thought he was (7)_____.

The men were found the following day by the Chamonix mountain (8)_____ team, who had been sent up the mountain to find two other climbers who had also disappeared. All six were then lifted off the mountain by helicopter and taken to Chamonix hospital, where doctors (9)_____ to get Mr Haywood's heart beating again (10)_____ in time. A doctor said there was a good chance that he would (11)_____, and explained that the effects of the extreme cold would have helped to (12)_____ serious brain damage.

So far this year there has been a (13)_____ number of emergencies in Chamonix. The mountains around the town have (14)_____ 93 lives and left 726 people injured. Eleven people are still (15)_____.

	A	B	C	D
0	recovered	relived	recuperated	revived
1	party	set	crew	pack
2	clean	clear	pure	calm
3	didn't manage	couldn't	didn't succeed	didn't achieve
4	possibility	choice	occasion	opportunity
5	temperature	warmth	fever	hot
6	caught	held	trapped	closed
7	die	died	death	dead
8	rescue	release	delivery	repair
9	could	managed	achieved	succeeded
10	only	simply	just	merely
11	save	repair	recover	rescue
12	avoid	prevent	escape	obstruct
13	record	greatest	largest	highest
14	claimed	removed	killed	died
15	away	absent	out	missing

G Language study 3

Read these articles from a newspaper. Put the verb in brackets into the active or passive. Use the tense that is shown at the beginning of each passage.

1 Present continuous

CHAOS ON M25 SET TO CONTINUE

The chaos on London's orbital motorway, the M25, looks set to continue for a few weeks. Important repairs (1)__________(carry out) between junctions 18 and 19 at the moment, and traffic (2)__________ (divert) along other routes. At the M40 intersection, a bridge (3)__________(widen) and this (4)__________(cause) long delays and tailbacks of up to 5 miles. Motorists (5)__________ (advise) to avoid the area if at all possible.

2 Present perfect

FOREST FIRES SWEEP ACROSS FRANCE

In the last few days, uncontrollable forest fires (1)__________(sweep) across the South of France. Thousands of square miles of trees (2)__________(burn) and hundreds of homes (3)__________(destroy). So far no one (4)__________(kill) but scores of people (5)__________(injure) trying to fight the blaze. The fires are close to many of the popular holiday resorts and tourists (6)__________(warn) not to travel to the affected areas. A number of tour operators in England (7)__________(cancel) holidays to the region and alternative destinations (8)__________ (arrange).

3 Past perfect

BESTON MANOR BREAK-IN

Thieves last night broke into Beston Manor, the home of Lady Trumpdon, and made off with paintings worth more than £1m. 'I woke up because the alarm (1)__________(set off), and I knew something was wrong. I went down to the gallery, but by the time I got there the thieves (2)__________(take) what they wanted. I was horrified to see that they (3)__________(steal) three valuable Old Masters, and that they (4)__________(break) some valuable vases in their hurry to escape.' A tearful Lady Trumpdon told reporters that there (5)__________ (be) several previous break-ins, but that this was the first time that anything really valuable (6)__________ (take).

4 Past continuous

BOMB SUSPECT ARRESTED

Patrick Mallory, who escaped from prison last year while he (1)__________(transfer) from Belfast, was arrested last night as he (2)__________(try) to leave the country. A police spokesman said he (3)__________(hold) in Horseferry Road police station, and (4)__________(question) by detectives from the Special Branch. The spokesman said that Mallory's home (5)__________(search) and that two other men, who had been staying with Mallory at the time of the arrest, (6)__________(help) police with their enquiries.

5 Simple present

RNLI APPEAL

The Royal National Lifeboat Institute urgently (1)__________(need) funds to be able to continue the emergency help we (2)__________(provide) for sailors and fishermen in distress. Every year thousands of distress and emergency calls (3)__________(answer) by our volunteers, and we (4)__________(go) out to sea in all weathers to help boats in distress. We are a charitable organization, and (5)__________ (not give) any funds by the government. We (6)__________(support) only by voluntary contributions from members of the public, and your help (7)__________(need) so that we can continue our important work.

6 Simple past

SURGEONS SAVE BOY'S ARM

An 11-year-old schoolboy from Leicester (1)__________(lose) an arm yesterday afternoon while playing with some friends at Trent Farm. The boy, Peter Ridge, (2)__________(fall) into some farm machinery, and his arm (3)__________(tear off) above the elbow. He (4)__________(take) to hospital, where surgeons (5)__________(work) throughout the night and (6)__________(sew) the arm back on. This morning his condition (7)__________(say) to be satisfactory.

UNIT 18

A Personality test

Do the personality test and find out what kind of person you are. Do you agree with the results?

Personality test

How outgoing are you?

Do you love attention or do you prefer to stay hidden in the shade? Find out with our quiz

Part One

If you had to work in the retail trade would you prefer:
- A to deal directly with the general public?
- B to work in an office dealing with the store's purchases?

When buying a new car what would you choose:
- A a red model?
- B a dark green model?

You want to redecorate your lounge. Would you pick:
- A a bright, colourful pattern?
- B a duller design in pale or pastel shades?

Given the choice, would you prefer to go to:
- A a lively party?
- B a quiet dinner with a good old friend?

Do you feel more confident:
- A dealing with a situation which calls for quick decisions?
- B handling a situation where you are going to have time to think things over first?

Which do you prefer:
- A a slapstick comedy where you can join in the laughter with a crowd of others?
- B a more subtle comedy where the humour may give you some food for thought?

If someone insults you do you:
- A insult them back?
- B go away and plan revenge?

If driving behind a slow motorist, would you:
- A overtake – whether you were in a hurry or not?
- B stay behind provided you were not in a hurry?

After a hard day's work would you rather read:
- A a light romance or an exciting detective story?
- B a long, serious novel?

Do you spend most of the weekend:
- A with lots of other people?
- B by yourself or with one or two close companions?

Part Two

Tick the statements that apply to you:
- I'm often the centre of attention when I go to parties.
- I'm a good leader.
- I have a wide circle of friends.
- I like going out dancing.
- I'm often asked for my opinion.
- I get on with children.

- I sometimes enjoy playing silly games.
- I take part in some amateur theatricals sometimes.
- I like organizing social events.
- I enjoy talking to strangers.
- I often make snap decisions.
- I prefer using the telephone to letter writing.
- I enjoy practical jokes.
- I'm more confident than most.
- I seldom worry about the future.
- I tend to be impulsive.
- I'm a doer, not a thinker.

Add up the number of statements you ticked in Part Two and add to this one point for every A ticked in Part One – Bs score nil.

24 points or more:
You have a powerful, outgoing personality that others may find rather overpowering at times. Try not to be quite so pushy.

18–23 points:
You have an outgoing personality which is probably just about right – impressing others without overpowering them at all.

12–17 points:
You are able to switch from an outgoing to a more reserved approach. But beware – people may think you're insincere.

5–11 points:
You are rather reserved but you still make a good impression, probably appearing sympathetic.

Fewer than 5 points:
You do tend to be rather too quiet and may not impress other people sufficiently.

B Vocabulary

Find words in the test that mean:

1 difficult to explain or describe ________
2 punishment for someone who has hurt or injured you ________
3 be very rude to someone ________
4 acting without thinking first ________
5 forward, demanding attention ________
6 not genuine, pretending ________
7 understanding/concerned ________

Now can you match the words on the left with their opposites on the right? Draw lines between the pairs.

outgoing	light
thinker	dull
bright	quiet
lively	doer
serious	reserved

C Reading

Read the article about Amy Irving, actress and former wife of director Steven Spielberg. Seven sentences have been removed from the article. Choose from sentences A–H the one that fits each gap (1–6). There is one extra sentence which you do not need. There is an example at the beginning (0).

When actress Amy Irving first came to Santa Fe 15 years ago, she lived high on a mountainside in a small house that was heated with wood. **0** *E* Her attitude was aggressive – the result of being an independent, talented woman who was struggling against the curse of fame by association.

As a gifted young stage actress, Amy constantly found herself identified as the daughter of the late theatre director Jules Irving and actress Priscilla Pointer. **1** ____ When Amy and Spielberg had their son Max, and married in Santa Fe in 1985, Amy was thrown into 'the role of the politician's wife'. **2** ____ Now, Amy is in Santa Fe once again, relaxing on the terrace of the home she bought the year she split from Spielberg for good. **3** ____ Inside the house, Willie Nelson blasts from the stereo. Within Amy's face the same impossibly blue eyes flash, and her voice is still deep when she speaks, her diction still perfect from years of formal dramatic training. **4** ____ The most obvious difference is her hair, the chaos of the curls replaced by a short and chic cut. Amy almost looks as if she has emerged from a cocoon – of hair, dress and attitude – and changed into an elegant butterfly version of her former self.

'Bruno (the new love in her life) has redesigned me,' Amy says, with the quiet smile that comes every time she mentions the Brazilian film director, the father of her second son, five-year-old Gabriel. **5** ____ More recently they have collaborated again, as executive co-producers and as director and actress on *Carried Away*. But, although important, success isn't everything for the actress. **6** ____ As she settles into a sofa, at peace with the environment, Amy offers a living illustration of the truth she has spoken.

A 'When you look at the sunset here, or the stars in the sky at night, suddenly some movie-deal seems such a silly, minor thing in your life,' says Amy.
B And, despite her success in the films *Carrie*, *Yentl* and *Crossing Delancey*, the world still preferred to see her as the girlfriend of famous director Steven Spielberg.
C 'It's been really intense – Bruno hasn't stopped since January and has missed this trip to Santa Fe because', Amy says, 'he's too busy working'.
D And yet, as Amy leans against a post on the terrace, the overall effect is one of change and transformation.
E At that time, her hair was an explosion of curls, and her wardrobe was full of denim and flannel.
F Then, when she and Spielberg divorced three and a half years later, she felt herself melting into 'nonexistence'.
G Amy and Bruno fell in love when he directed her in a film called 'A Show of Force', a thriller that Amy admits was not a professional success for either of them.
H Behind her can be seen the unearthly light falling across the Jemez mountains in the spectacular way that has always drawn her to this part of the world.

D Language study 1

Rewrite these sentences using *in case*, *if* or *whether*.

Example:
Take your umbrella *in case* it rains.
I'll take my umbrella *if* it's raining.
I don't know *whether* to take my umbrella or not.

> ***Remember:*** *in case* introduces something that may possibly happen later and means *as a precaution against*.

1 Tell me the telephone number again because I might forget.
2 We can stay at the Ritz hotel, provided that they have a room.
3 We'll go to the theatre as we'll probably have time.
4 I'll take my credit card as we might spend more than we expected to.
5 Should we stay for the whole week or not? We really don't know.
6 We'll order a taxi to take us to the station. It might be raining!
7 We'll put our valuables in the hotel safe. They might get stolen otherwise!
8 Should we go by train or bus? It's difficult to decide.

E Phrasal verbs

Rewrite these sentences using the word in bold.

Example:
'Go towards the bus station on the left,' the old man said.
make
The old man told me *to make for* the bus station on the left.

1 'Have you invented this story or not?' Susan asked Jim.
made
Susan asked Jim whether he ______________ or not.

2 'Please write a cheque payable to 'City Bank',' said the cashier.
make
The cashier asked me to ______________ to 'City Bank'.

3 'You'd better forget your quarrel now children,' said the twins' mother.
make
The twins' mother told them ______________ after their quarrel.

4 It was impossible for us to see what the children were doing at the bottom of the garden.
make
We ______________ what the children were doing at the bottom of the garden.

5 You should have gone in the direction of the station, not the town centre!
made
It would have been better if you ______________ the station, not the town centre.

F Language study 2

Which would you use with the following words: *a*, *an*, or *some*?

________	advice	________	office
________	homework	________	exercise
________	furniture	________	sofa
________	work	________	baggage
________	assistant	________	news
________	help	________	newspaper
________	information	________	job
________	handbag		

Now choose five of the words above and use them in sentences of your own.

1 ______________________________
2 ______________________________
3 ______________________________
4 ______________________________
5 ______________________________

G Use of English

Complete the text with the correct form of the words in capitals. There is an example at the beginning (0).

People often dream about being rich and (0) *famous* but in reality this is not as (1)__________ as it seems. In fact, it can be quite the opposite! Just having a (2)__________ or handsome face which everyone recognizes causes (3)__________ problems. If you go out, one (4)__________ move can result in being mobbed by (5)__________ fans, so you have to be (6)__________ to hide your identity at all times, if you do not want this to happen. Bodyguards can be (7)__________ in that they can protect you from (8)__________ encounters with the public but, eventually you realize the (9)__________ truth: you are no longer (10)__________ to do exactly what you would like to!

0 FAME
1 DESIRE
2 BEAUTY
3 END
4 CARE
5 ENTHUSIASM
6 CARE
7 HELP
8 HARM
9 PAIN
10 ABILITY

H Language study 3

What advice would you give in this situation?

You'd better put your raincoat on.
You'd better not go out just yet.

Give advice using you'd better (not) for these situations.

> ***Remember:*** after *had better (not)* we use the infinitive without *to*.

1 Your friend has had too much to eat already.

____

2 Your colleague is falling asleep during an important meeting.

____

3 You think your friend should tell his parents what he's done.

____

4 Your husband/wife seems very run down and tired.

____

5 Your son/daughter has some important exams in a few weeks' time.

____

6 You don't want your daughter to forget her passport when she goes on holiday.

____

7 Your friend is driving too quickly on a wet road.

____

8 The fuel gauge on your friend's car indicates empty.

____

9 Your brother's hair is too long and he has an interview next week.

____

10 Your friend is catching a train at 6.00 and it's 5.45 now.

____

UNIT 19

A Reading

Read the text and choose the best answer in 1–7.

NO PLACE LIKE HOME

All over the country young people are entering a world of homelessness and poverty, according to a recent report by the housing group, Shelter.

Nearly 150,000 young people aged between sixteen and twenty-five will become homeless this year, says Shelter. Some of the young homeless may sleep out in the open in such places as 'cardboard city' in London, where people of all ages sleep in the open air in their only homes – cardboard boxes. Others may find accommodation in shelters run by voluntary organizations or get a place in a hostel, which gives them board for up to ten weeks.

But who are these people? Those seeking a roof over their heads are mostly not runaways but 'throwaways' – people who have been thrown out of their homes or forced to leave because of parental divorce, an unsympathetic step-parent or one of many other reasons.

Take the case of one sixteen-year-old schoolgirl we shall call Alice. She did not come from a poor home and had just passed her exams with good results. The Shelter team met her in an overnight hostel where she was sitting down doing her Physics homework. It turned out that her parents had thrown her out of her home for no other reason that she wanted to do Science Advanced Level exams – which her parents refused her permission to do, saying that sciences were unladylike!

Shelter says that the Government's laws do nothing to help these youngsters.

Rising rents, a shortage of cheap housing and a cut in benefits for young people under the age of twenty-five are causing a national problem, according to Shelter. The recent changes in the benefit laws mean that someone aged between sixteen and twenty-five gets less than older people and they can only claim state help if they prove that they left home for a good reason.

Shelter believes that because of the severe cuts in benefits to young people, more and more are being forced to sleep on the streets. Shelter also points out that if you are homeless, you can't get a job because employers will not take on someone without a permanent address; and if you can't get a job, you are homeless because you don't have any money to pay for accommodation. It's an impossible situation.

1 According to a recent report by Shelter, it appears that
- A nearly 150,000 young people are living out in the open.
- B young homeless people live in places like 'cardboard city'.
- C more and more young people all over the world are finding themselves homeless.
- D hostels are too full to offer accommodation to homeless young people.

2 Most young people find themselves without a roof over their heads because
- A they have run away from home.
- B they do not want to live with a divorced parent.
- C circumstances make it impossible for them to live at home.
- D they have thrown away any chance of living at home by behaving badly.

3 Why was Alice turned out of her home?
- A She didn't want to study for her Advanced Level exams.
- B She had not obtained high marks in her exams.
- C She refused to do her homework in the evenings.
- D Her parents didn't agree with what she wanted to do.

4 According to the text, what are *benefits*?
- A gifts of food and clothing
- B laws about distributing money
- C subsidies for those in need
- D extra wages for part-time workers

5 The changes in the system of benefits mean that
- A young people cannot claim money unless they are under sixteen or over twenty-five.
- B anyone under twenty-five and not living at home will receive help with food and accommodation.
- C young people do not receive as much money as those over twenty-five.
- D The under twenty-fives can claim money only if they have left home.

6 According to Shelter, once young people have been forced onto the streets,
- A they will find it difficult to find work.
- B their benefits will be severely cut.
- C they will never go back home again.
- D they will encourage their friends to do the same.

7 The article has been written to
- A help Shelter solve the problems of the homeless.
- B increase awareness of the problems facing young people.
- C warn young people not to be too eager to leave home.
- D persuade the government to take action to help the young.

B Language study 1

Rewrite the two sentences in 1–8 to make one 'unreal' conditional sentence, showing both *cause* and *result*.

Example:
I got married. I left home.
If I hadn't got married, I wouldn't have left home.

> ***Remember:*** for the *cause* use *if* + *Past perfect tense*
> for the *result* use the *Perfect conditional tense.*

1 I had a baby. I gave up my job.

____

____

2 My husband lost his job. We came back to England.

____

____

3 My husband found another job. We stayed in England.

____

____

4 I had another baby. I got a part-time job.

____

____

5 We saved some money. We were able to buy a house.

____

____

6 We bought a large four-bedroom house. We found it difficult to make ends meet.

____

____

7 We worked hard for many years. We finished paying for the house.

____

____

8 We won the lottery. Our problems disappeared!

____

____

C Phrasal verbs

Rewrite these sentences using the word in bold.

Example:
Sylvia and Peter's relationship is not very successful.
get
Sylvia and Peter don't *get on with* each other at all.

1 I never know how my boss manages to do so little work.
away
How does my boss manage to ______________ so little work?

2 Martin can never find the time to do his homework.
gets
Martin hardly ever ______________ his homework.

3 Would you like to have a drink with me tonight?
getting
What about ______________ a drink tonight?

4 I'm not an early riser myself!
up
I can't stand ______________ in the morning!

5 The new manager doesn't seem to be able to explain his ideas to his staff.
across
The new manager is not very good ______________ to his staff.

6 It took Sally ages to recover from her illness.
get
Sally ______________ her illness.

7 The cold weather is really depressing me at the moment.
getting
The cold weather is ______________ at the moment.

8 The bicycle my father lost was returned to him last night.
got
My father lost his bicycle but he ______________ last night.

D Vocabulary 1

What names do we give to the following professions? In some cases more than one word may be possible.

Example:
a person who makes bread *a baker*

1 studies history ______________
2 plays the piano ______________
3 teaches ______________
4 looks after the sick ______________
5 advises people on legal matters ______________
6 plays a musical instrument ______________
7 goes up in a spacecraft ______________
8 prepares meals for a living ______________
9 designs buildings ______________
10 flies an aeroplane ______________

E Vocabulary 2

Now write sentences explaining what the following people do for a living (you may need your dictionary to help you).

1 A dentist ______________________________
____

2 A joiner ______________________________
____

3 A plumber ______________________________
____

4 A postman ______________________________
____

5 An accountant ______________________________
____

6 A dress designer ______________________________
____

7 A waiter/waitress ______________________________
____

8 A publisher ______________________________
____

F Language study 2

Make sentences of your own using *It's time...* + the simple past to show that something should be done.

Example:
My bicycle is falling to pieces.
It's time I bought a new bicycle.

1 It's 9.30 and Bill hasn't done his homework yet.
2 The grass at the front of the house needs cutting.
3 Michael is 39 and he's still living with his parents!
4 I think we should go home now.
5 I've been working non-stop for the last three hours.
6 This government's policies aren't very popular.
7 The company's very short-staffed.
8 The remote control for the TV's broken again.

G Language study 3

Complete the conversation with the correct form of the verb in brackets.

Rosy: Hi, Sue! How are you?

Sue: Fine, thanks. And you?

Rosy: I'm exhausted. We (1)________(work) non-stop for the last few weeks. If I (2)________(not get) a break soon, I (3)________(go) crazy!

Sue: It sounds as if it's time you (4)________(have) a holiday! Are you going away this summer?

Rosy: Well, if we (5)________(can) afford it, we (6)________(go) to Spain.

Sue: Didn't you do that last year?

Rosy: We were going to. In fact, if the children (7)________(not go) on a Scout Camp, we (8)________(spend) three weeks in Spain, but we went to Cornwall instead.

Sue: Where (9)________(you/like) to go, if you (10)________(have) the money?

Rosy: Oh, Australia. I (11)________(always/want) to go there! Look, I must dash. It's time I (12)________(be) at work!

Sue: All right! Nice to talk to you. See you soon and don't work too hard.

Rosy: I'll try not to! Take care!

H Vocabulary 3

Divide the words below into five groups according to which prefix you need to use to make them negative.

necessary	satisfied	tolerant	religious
accurate	polite	regular	certain
orderly	lucky	convenient	possible
resistible	sensitive	friendly	pleased

im-	un-	dis-	ir-	in-

Now use one of the words you have made to complete the sentences below. More than one word may be suitable.

1 It is very ___________ to make rude gestures at people!

2 I'm afraid the patient's heartbeat seems to be rather ___________

3 The twins can't stop eating chocolate – they find it ___________!

4 Walking under a ladder, and Friday the 13th are considered ___________ in this country.

5 The teacher was very ___________ with the homework the students had handed in.

6 Could I call you back later? It's rather ___________ at the moment.

7 People who live in big cities are said to be cold and ___________.

8 The passengers jumped off the train in a somewhat ___________ fashion.

I Writing

You have seen this advertisement for a job in the local paper and you would like some more details about it.

Read the advert and the comments you have made, then write a letter of 120–180 words to the Personnel Manager giving some information about yourself. Say why you might be interested in the job and ask for the details you need.

> **OFFICE JUNIOR**
>
> *needed for interesting work in small business in the city.*
>
> *Attractive wages offered to the right person.*
>
> Write with details to:
> Multiware Complex,
> 15, High Road,
> Princeton W11 9HR

Notes to include:
What type of work?
What kind of business?
Hours of work?
Pay?
What kind of 'right' person?

UNIT 20

A Reading 1

Read the text. Seven sentences have been removed. Choose from sentences A–H the one that fits each gap (1–6). There is one extra sentence which you do not need. There is an example at the beginning (0).

RUINING THE RUINS

Acid rain is now a familiar problem in the industrialized countries in Europe. Gases like sulphur dioxide and nitrogen oxide are produced by power stations and cars. [0 *F*]

Acid rain is also capable of dissolving some rocks, and buildings made of soft rock, such as limestone, are particularly badly affected. The acid rain attacks the rock, and so carvings and statues are eroded more quickly.

[1] According to a report in the *New Scientist*, acid rain is being blamed for the rapid decay of ancient ruins in Mexico. The old limestone buildings in places like Chichen Itza, Tulum and Palenque are wearing away very quickly indeed. These sites are the remains of the buildings built by the Mayas between 250 BC and AD 900, and the spectacular ruins of Mayan civilization are visited by thousands of tourists every year.

But those ruins are in danger of being seriously damaged by pollution. At many sites the stone has been covered with a layer of black substance like tar. [2]

Scientists estimate that about one millimetre of stone is worn away every twelve years. [3] The acid rain is said to be caused by pollution from oil wells in the gulf of Mexico. Car exhaust gases are also a problem. Local volcanic eruptions make the problem even worse. Nevertheless, with enough money and effort, researchers say that many of the problems could be solved and the rate of erosion reduced. [4]

Mexico's current lack of funds is also partly due to oil. The country has rich oil fields and a few years ago, when oil was expensive, Mexico was selling large quantities of oil to the USA and earning a lot of money. [5] However, the price of oil then dropped, and Mexico has been left owing enormous sums of money and with not enough income from oil sales to pay back the loans. [6]

A At others the painted surfaces inside temples are lifting and flaking off and the stone is being eaten away.

B That is enough to have caused some of the ancient carvings to become seriously damaged already.

C So unless the price of oil rises, it is unlikely that Mexico will be able to afford to clean up the pollution and save its Mayan ruins from destruction.

D These measures would reduce the pollution, but would not stop it completely.

E The government was therefore able to borrow huge sums of money from banks around the world, thinking they would have no problem repaying their debts.

F They dissolve in rainwater and this makes acid rain, which damages trees, rivers and streams.

G The problem, however, is not just a European one.

H However, the Mexican government does not have enough money to do the work, and needs to spend what money it has on the Mexican people.

B Vocabulary

Find words in the text which mean:

1 to become part of a liquid ________
2 shapes or designs cut out of wood or stone ________
3 damaged by slow and gradual rubbing or friction ________
4 extremely old ________
5 old buildings that have fallen into decay ________
6 wonderful to look at ________
7 made smaller ________
8 amounts of money that are owed to someone ________

C Use of English 1

Rewrite these sentences using the word in bold.

1 The musical was so successful that all the tickets were sold.
success
The musical ______________ that all the tickets were sold.

2 I haven't seen my aunt for ages.
last
It's ______________ my aunt.

3 The only reason he crashed was because he was speeding.
would
If he hadn't ______________ have crashed.

4 They crossed the Atlantic in three days.
them
It ______________ cross the Atlantic.

5 She isn't nearly old enough to play in the championship.
young
She ______________ to play in the championship.

6 There's no doubt that the thief had a key.
must
The ______________ a key.

7 Learning new words isn't easy for me.
find
I ______________ new words.

8 The boss said it was Jane's fault that the letter had been lost.
blamed
The boss ______________ the letter.

9 Could I borrow your bike this weekend?
me
Would ______________ your bike this weekend?

10 He looked after his mother well.
care
He ______________ his mother.

D Use of English 2

Read the text and think of ONE word which best fits each space. There is an example at the beginning (0).

Many tourists (0) *who* visit Central America find (1)________ surprising to learn that the Mayas still live there. (2)________ it is true that their ancient civilization came to an end when their country was taken (3)________ by the Spanish conquistadors, the Mayan people carried (4)________ living in the area. Today there are an estimated 1.2 million Mayas (5)________ live in southern Mexico, and many other areas of Central America states have large Mayan populations as (6)________ .

Many of their stories and art forms have remained unchanged over time, and today, women weave clothing and carpets that have signs and symbols that are the (7)________ as those found in ancient temples. The different patterns and symbols on these brightly coloured clothes (8)________ only look attractive, (9)________ can also communicate important information such (10)________ marital status.

(11)________ though the majority (12)________ the Mayas are now Catholic, many of the festivals that they (13)________ part in are a mixture of the old rituals that their ancestors (14)________ to practise and more modern Christian elements. It was perhaps the Mayas' ability to adapt and change that made (15)________ possible for them to survive to the present day.

E Use of English 3

Read the text and decide which word, A, B, C or D, best fits each space. There is an example at the beginning (0).

An American professor who has studied the Mayas has (0) *come* up with a new theory about the sudden end of their empire. (1)_____ to Professor Richard Hansen, an archaeologist at the University of California, the (2)_____ of the Mayan civilisation in Central America was (3)_____ about by the Mayas themselves.

'Their object was to display their (4)_____ and power by making their buildings and decoration as beautiful as possible. This (5)_____ using large quantities of lime, which they put on the walls to make them smooth. Unfortunately, the creation of lime is a process which requires intense heat, and they therefore (6)_____ to cut down huge numbers of trees. This affected the quality of the soil, and it became almost impossible to farm.'

Professor Hansen, who has (7)_____ returned from an excavation in the El Mirador region of northern Guatemala, (8)_____ a meeting of archaeologists in Philadelphia that the Mayas, having (9)_____ this mistake in the 3rd century, repeated it 600 years later, at which time it proved fatal. Increasing food (10)_____ among the Mayas created a Central American equivalent of the Peloponnesian War which ravaged (11)_____ Greece. However, (12)_____ the Greek civil war, which only (13)_____ for 27 years, the Mayan wars (14)_____ on for many centuries and left many of their great cities and temples in (15)_____ .

	A	B	C	D
0	A brought	B come	C found	D stood
1	A Referring	B Relating	C According	D Respecting
2	A collapse	B drop	C crash	D stop
3	A made	B came	C turned	D brought
4	A wealth	B fortune	C salary	D cash
5	A depended	B needed	C requested	D involved
6	A obliged	B forced	C must	D had
7	A still	B just	C already	D yet
8	A explained	B suggested	C claimed	D told
9	A done	B had	C taken	D made
10	A lack	B shortages	C droughts	D failures
11	A antique	B old	C past	D ancient
12	A unless	B apart	C without	D unlike
13	A stayed	B spent	C longed	D lasted
14	A ran	B went	C came	D brought
15	A injuries	B damages	C spoils	D ruins

F Reading 2

Read the information below about a large charity, The Salmon Foundation (A), and the three groups (B,C,D) which are applying for money. For questions 1–14, choose from A–D. There is an example at the beginning (0).

Which section (A–D) mentions

a group that sends well-qualified people abroad?	0	*C*
an organization that does not try to make money?	1	
a group whose members would come from different countries?	2	
a group that has no direct experience of the project they are planning?	3	
an organization that has paid part of the cost of large projects?	4	
an organization that tries to get people from different countries to know each other better?	5	
a project that will do some research into food?	6	
a project that will help poor people directly?	7	
a group that will continue work that has already been started?	8	
a group whose project will be partly paid for by the local government?	9	
a group whose project cannot be paid for by the local government?	10	
an organization that will make a new product?	11	
a group that has already been offered a loan?	12	
a group that will ask different people for money in the future?	13	
a project whose work may be of value to large corporations?	14	

A

THE SALMON FOUNDATION

The Salmon Foundation is a non-profit-making charity founded by Howard Salmon in 1985. Every year the organization gives out an award of $500,000.

The aims of the award scheme are:

- to promote international understanding through scientific research.
- to encourage the development of new products for the benefit of all people.
- to extend cultural ties between countries.

The Salmon Foundation prefers to give only one large award per year rather than a number of small ones; in the past it has given awards to help pay for a part of very large projects.

B

THE MAYAN SITE GROUP

Project:

to carry out further excavations at Mayan sites; to research history of Mayan culture; to work on ways of protecting old buildings from pollution.

Background:

- The group consists of professors from eleven universities around the world.
- The Mexican government cannot fund the project.
- The group requires $300,000 for the first year, then may find money from elsewhere.
- Many Mayan sites are not fully excavated and many buildings are being damaged by pollution.

C

The Water Well Group

Project:

to develop a solar-powered pump for water wells; to manufacture the pumps and install them on farms in Africa and South America.

Background:

- The group is part of 'Volunteers Overseas', an organization which sends science graduates to help in developing countries.
- The group has not done a project like this before.
- At least $700,000 is needed; one large bank has promised to lend $200,000.
- The first pumps will go to areas often affected by famine.

D

Panda Protection Group

Project:

to set up a safe area in Northern China for eight pandas; to start a breeding programme; to research into the diet of pandas.

Background:

- The project would involve scientists from five countries.
- Pandas are an endangered species and are in need of special protection.
- The Chinese government will give the group necessary land and will pay for one of the scientists.
- The group needs a further $200,000 to set up the project.

G Use of English 4

Complete the text with the correct form of the words in capitals. There is an example at the beginning (0).

Many years ago, archaeology was about making (0) *spectacular* discoveries and finding buried treasure. Now, however, it has become a more (1)________ subject, and archaeologists are becoming increasingly (2)________ in finding out more about the lives of ordinary people rather than the (3)________ lives of kings and emperors.

Much of the work of an archaeologist can be tedious and (4)________ ; 99% of archaeology is concerned with reading, excavating, recording and classifying, and, unlike the world of Indiana Jones, it is neither thrilling nor (5)________. However, the real (6)________ of archaeology comes through an (7)________ stream of new (8)________, any one of which may alter the way we look at history. Even the smallest piece of pottery, however (9)________ it may appear at first glance, can change our whole (10)________ of things that happened in the past.

0 SPECTACLE
1 SCIENCE
2 INTEREST
3 DRAMA
4 REPEAT
5 DANGER
6 EXCITE
7 END
8 DISCOVER
9 IMPORTANCE
10 UNDERSTAND

H Phrasal verbs

Write the missing words from the sentences in the wordcomb to find the hidden message.

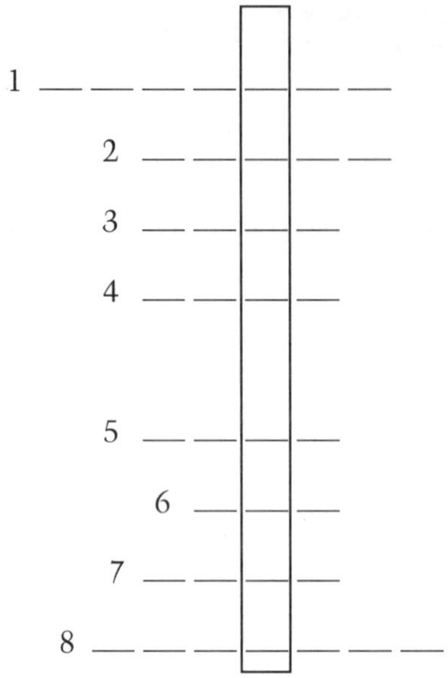

1 I was born in America, but I was ________ up in Canada, and I went to school there. (7)
2 As soon as she found out her boyfriend was seeing someone else, she ________ off the engagement. (5)
3 If you're free this afternoon, why don't you ________ in on Mrs Williamson on your way home? (4)
4 He didn't want to tell his father where he had been, so he ________ up a story about having to stay late at school. (4)
5 He ________ for her as soon as he saw her – it was love at first sight. (4)
6 If we don't get to a garage soon, we're going to ________ out of petrol. (3)
7 You're at the station, are you? OK, I'll come over and ________ you up in about 10 minutes. (4)
8 I expect you've been ________ forward to finishing this workbook for ages. Well, now you have! (7)

PROGRESS TEST 4

A Vocabulary cloze

Decide which word, A, B, C, or D, best fits each space. There is an example at the beginning (0).

The ruins of Pompeii

In AD 79, Mount Vesuvius (0) *erupted* , sending out a huge cloud of dust and rock that darkened the sky. It came without warning, and the (1)______ of the explosion was so great that it was felt from hundreds of miles away.

In the town of Pompeii, at the foot of the volcano, the inhabitants picked up whatever belongings they (2)______ carry and (3)______ the open countryside. In the terrible storm that followed, dust and rock from the volcano rained down onto the town, filling the streets with deep layers of ash and poisonous gas, (4)______ it impossible for the people to (5)______ . The town of Pompeii was completely (6)______ by the rain of death, and (7)______ lost to the world for centuries.

Excavation work did not begin (8)______ 1748, when Rocco Alcubierre found some wall paintings while he was digging at the site. In the years that followed, archaeologists realized that they had (9)______ one of the most astonishing ruins of all time. Almost everything in Pompeii had been (10)______ preserved. Several houses still had their roofs, and inside the furniture and the decorations were (11)______ as they had been centuries (12)______ . There were also the remains of over 2,000 people. Some of the (13)______ had made the mistake of sheltering in their cellars, where they were killed by poisonous gases from the volcano. Others had been (14)______ from escaping, and in the prison were men who had been chained to the wall and (15)______ to die.

0	A erupted	B ejected	C emerged	D expanded
1	A energy	B fuel	C power	D efficiency
2	A managed	B succeeded	C achieved	D could
3	A made up	B made out	C made over	D made for
4	A having	B leaving	C making	D turning
5	A get down	B get over	C get away	D get on
6	A damaged	B hurt	C collapsed	D destroyed
7	A lay	B lied	C laid	D lain
8	A by	B until	C for	D since
9	A come up	B come across	C come over	D come on
10	A exactly	B perfectly	C accurately	D precisely
11	A same	B alike	C just	D similar
12	A earlier	B previous	C former	D preceding
13	A injured	B victims	C sufferers	D deaths
14	A avoided	B blocked	C arrested	D prevented
15	A deserted	B abandoned	C left	D rejected

B Open cloze

Think of ONE word which best fits each space. There is an example at the beginning (0).

School Blaze

I have always been afraid (0) *of* fires because when I was eight years old, my boarding school burned down. Even now, I clearly remember waking up in the big bedroom late at night. Something (1)________ to be wrong, but I did not know what it was. I got (2)________ of bed and walked to the door and put my hand on the glass. It was hot, and (3)________ though there were no alarms or bells, it was clear that the building was (4)________ fire.

There were about twelve (5)________ us in the room, but as the eldest, I had to make sure that everyone was safe. I walked round the room telling everyone they (6)________ better get out at once. Fortunately we were all (7)________ to practising fire drills, so everyone knew (8)________ to do. We (9)________ our way down a series of iron ladders to the ground, and all (10)________ to get down safely. (11)________ soon as we got round to the front of the building, we saw how bad it was. The flames were hundreds of metres high and reached up into the night sky. The fire brigade was called, but (12)________ the time they arrived there was very (13)________ they could do and the building was completely destroyed. One boy was killed in the fire, but there is no doubt that many more would (14)________ died if we (15)________ not practised fire drills regularly.

C Key word transformations

Rewrite the sentences using the word in bold.

1 The smoke from the volcano was visible from miles away.
be
The smoke from the volcano _______________ from miles away.

2 John's taking his driving licence on holiday because he might decide to hire a car.
case
John's taking his driving licence on holiday _______________ hire a car.

3 There's no doubt that the prisoner who escaped had a key to the gates.
must
The prisoner who escaped _______________ a key to the gates.

4 It's really important you don't arrive late.
better
You _______________ late.

5 Our two sons have a good relationship.
get
Our two sons _______________ other.

6 You're nearly 35, so I really think you ought to get married.
got
You're nearly 35, so _______________ married.

7 I hope the builders will finish before we come back from holiday.
finished
I hope the builders _______________ the time we come back from holiday.

8 The prize money enabled Sally to buy a new car.
possible
The money _______________ to buy a new car

9 I didn't phone because I didn't realize you were in.
if
I would _______________ known you were in.

10 I'm not sure if she is lying or not.
not
I don't know _______________ she's telling the truth.

D Word formation

Complete the text with the correct form of the words in capitals. There is an example at the beginning (0).

Getting it wrong

People have always had (0) *difficulty* predicting the future. One of the least (1)__________ forecasters was Lord Kelvin, who was President of an (2)__________ made up of the most important (3)__________ of the day, called the 'Royal Society'.

The (4)__________ of the radio in 1895 was one of the greatest (5)__________ of the 19th century, but Kelvin was not (6)__________ and simply said: 'Radio has no future'. He went on to make other wildly (7)__________ claims. Despite these (8)__________ mistakes, he continued to look into the future. (9)__________ before the Wright brothers' historic flight, he said: 'Heavier-than-air flying machines are (10)__________ .'

0 DIFFICULT
1 SUCCESS
2 ORGANIZE
3 SCIENCE
4 INVENT
5 ACHIEVE
6 IMPRESS
7 ACCURACY
8 EMBARRASS
9 SHORT
10 POSSIBILITY